Linguistic Landscaping
and the Pacific Region

Linguistic Landscaping and the Pacific Region

Colonization, Indigenous Identities, and Critical Discourse Theory

Diane Elizabeth Johnson

LEXINGTON BOOKS
Lanham • Boulder • New York • London

Published by Lexington Books
An imprint of The Rowman & Littlefield Publishing Group, Inc.
4501 Forbes Boulevard, Suite 200, Lanham, Maryland 20706
www.rowman.com

Epigraph from Linda Tuhiwai Smith, *Decolonizing Methodologies: Research and Indigenous Peoples*, second edition. Zed Books: 2012. Reprinted with permission.

British Library Cataloguing in Publication Information Available

Library of Congress Cataloging-in-Publication Data

Names: Johnson, Diane Elizabeth, 1951-2020, author.
Title: Linguistic landscaping and the Pacific Region : colonization, indigenous identities, and critical discourse theory / Diane Elizabeth Johnson.
Description: Lanham : Lexington Books, 2021. | Includes bibliographical references and index. | Summary: "In Linguistic Landscaping and the Pacific Region: Colonization, Indigenous Identities, and Critical Discourse Theory, Diane Elizabeth Johnson provides four case studies, each exploring the use of language in public spaces in an area of the Pacific in which colonization has played a major role: Hawai'i, Aotearoa/ New Zealand, New Caledonia, and Tahiti. Each of these studies is informed by critical discourse theory, a theory which highlights the ways in which hegemonic structures may be established, reinforced, and- particularly in times of crisis-contested and overturned. The book introduces the case studies in the context of a parallel introduction to the Pacific region, critical discourse theory, and research on linguistic landscapes. The critical discussion is accessible to students and others who are approaching these contexts and theories for the first time, while also providing locating the author's work in relation to existing scholarship. Johnson urges readers to listen carefully to the voices of indigenous peoples at a time when the danger of Western certainties has been fully exposed"— Provided by publisher.
Identifiers: LCCN 2021019087 (print) | LCCN 2021019088 (ebook) |
    ISBN 9781793611185 (cloth) | ISBN 9781793611192 (epub)
Subjects: LCSH: Pacific Area—Languages. | Endangered languages—Pacific Area. | Language revival—Pacific Area. | Language policy—Pacific Area.
Classification: LCC P40.5.E532 P337 2021 (print) | LCC P40.5.E532 (ebook) |
    DDC 306.44099—dc23
LC record available at https://lccn.loc.gov/2021019087
LC ebook record available at https://lccn.loc.gov/2021019088

Contents

Acknowledgments   vii

Introduction   ix

1   The Pacific Region: Colonization, Resistance, and the Linguistic Landscape   1

INTRODUCTION TO PART I: BRITAIN AND THE UNITED STATES: COLONIALISM AND EXPANSIONISM   **17**

2   The Hawaiian Kingdom: Mount Maunakea: Assertion, Resistance, and the *Mise en Abyme* Effect   19

3   Aotearoa/New Zealand: Tirau: A Twenty-First Century Colonial Fantasy Landscape   47

INTRODUCTION TO PART II: METROPOLITAN FRANCE: PACIFIC COLONIAL EXPANSIONISM   **69**

4   Assertion and Resistance in the Linguistic Landscape of Kanaky/New Caledonia   73

5   Pape'ete: A City at Sea   93

Conclusion: Signs of the Times   121

References   127

Index   141

About the Author   149

Acknowledgments

This project would not have been possible without the support and assistance of a number of people.

I would like to acknowledge the support of the Research Committee of the Division of Arts, Law, Psychology and Social Sciences (DALPS) at the University of Waikato for a research grant to help with the travel associated with the project.

I am indebted to a number of people in various parts of the world: Dr Anne-Laure Dotte (New Caledonia; Mme. Dorothy Lubin-Lévy and M. Tanemaruatoa Michel Arakino (Tahiti), and Dr. Richard Keaoopuaokalani NeSmith (Kingdom of Hawai'i) who generously gave their time and expertise to answer my questions, to guide my thinking, and to provide further possibilities for research pathways. My thanks too, to a number of other people in each of the research locations (whose identity cannot be revealed for ethical reasons) who showed a strong interest in the project and willingly engaged in research conversations during which they offered a range of differing perspectives and allowed a richer understanding of their countries.

I particularly wish to offer my sincere thanks to my friend, colleague, and mentor, Dr. Winifred Crombie (for her encouragement throughout this project and for her perceptive editorial comments on the manuscript as it evolved), to my research assistant Todd Stewart (for providing so much help with the gaining of permissions relating to the illustrations included in the book), to Dr. Tom Roa (for mentoring and cultural guidance over many years), and finally, and once again, Dr. Richard Keaoopuaokalani NeSmith (for so much in relation to the cultural and linguistic content of chapters 2 and 5).

Diane Johnson

Diane Johnson died shortly after completing the text of this book and it, therefore, stands as her final statement of belief.

Introduction

[T]he indigenous world view, the land and the people, have been radically transformed in the spatial image of the West. In other words, indigenous space has been colonized.

Linda Tuhiwai Smith,
Decolonizing methodologies, p. 51.

This book was written in 2019, the International Year of Indigenous Languages, a year in which the United Nations aimed to raise awareness of indigenous language endangerment and to establish a link between language, development, peace, and reconciliation. It is, therefore, particularly appropriate that the book is concerned with what the linguistic landscape (LL) of colonized areas of the Pacific can tell us about issues relating to power, loss, reclamation, and identity.

At the core of research on LL is the visibility, or otherwise, of a language or languages in public spaces, such as supermarkets, town squares, public buildings, or roadways. Are road signs, for example, all in one language or is more than one language represented? Where two or more languages are in evidence, is one of them more salient than others? It is not, however, only the presence or absence of written signs that is of interest to those involved in LL-centered research. They are also interested in the purpose of these signs (e.g., to provide information, to sell products, or to protest), who is responsible for them (e.g., local authorities, business owners, or local youths) and the contexts in which they appear. Of interest too are the people who move into and out of public spaces, people whose voices, together with, for example, background music, make up the soundscape which contributes to the overall semiotoscape. All of this adds to the richness of potential meanings and interpretations of the LL itself.

Much of the work in the area of LL to date has been conducted in contexts where there are multilingual and multicultural populations. This inevitably involves consideration of what messages are conveyed by the signage in relation to attitudes toward these populations. However, even though the Pacific islands are extraordinarily rich in linguistic and cultural diversity, very little LL-centered research has been conducted in the Pacific region. My aim in this book is, therefore, to approach LL-centered research from a Pacific perspective, conducting and reporting on studies in which issues relating, in particular, to colonization and indigeneity are highlighted. Each of these studies is explored in the context of critical discourse theory (CDT), a theory which highlights the ways in which hegemonic structures are established, reinforced, and, particularly in times of crisis, contested and overturned.

The book is divided into five chapters. The first provides an introduction to the study, discussing the history of the Pacific region in general terms and, more specifically, the impact of colonization on indigenous populations in the Pacific region. It discusses what is involved in LL-centered research, providing illustrative examples from Aotearoa/ New Zealand. It also introduces the case studies reported in chapters 2 through 5 in the context of the theoretical and methodological approaches adopted. Each of the next four chapters focuses on a study conducted in a Pacific country or region with which I am familiar: The Hawaiian Kingdom/Hawai'i; Aotearoa/New Zealand; Kanaky/New Caledonia; and Tahiti.[1] In each case, the primary focus is on the ways in which the LL examined relates to issues of indigeneity, colonization, and resistance. The Conclusion discusses how the four studies, taken together, throw light on the ways in which linguistic landscaping can contribute to our understanding of issues relating to colonization and indigenous identity in the Pacific region.

In writing this book, I have attempted to maintain a focus throughout on evidences in the LL of the impact of Western colonization on indigenous peoples in the Pacific region. Hence, I have not attempted to provide an account of the historical development of LL research or to discuss the wide variety of theories and methodologies with which it has been associated to date. Nor have I attempted to provide a discussion/review of arguments for and against the theoretical and methodological framework of the current work. Rather, largely for the benefit of readers who are unfamiliar with the literature, I have provided in the introductory chapter selected references to LL-focused research relevant to each of the case studies in subsequent chapters. I have sought to demonstrate the validity and usefulness of my own theoretical and methodological positioning through their application to these case studies.

In each of the four central chapters, an initial section provides an account of historical developments in the country/region concerned. These accounts are intended to be as factual as possible, avoiding the Eurocentric perspective that often pervades such narratives, and thus allowing for the emergence of indigenous perspectives. The length of these accounts is, I believe, justified in view of the importance of contextualizing the LL-focused material that follows in order to provide a framework for its interpretation.

NOTE

1. The place names commonly now used are, in three cases, preceded by the names generally preferred by the indigenous people of each area.

Chapter 1

The Pacific Region

Colonization, Resistance, and the Linguistic Landscape

The Pacific Ocean, covering approximately one third of the Earth's surface area, extends from the Arctic Ocean in the north to Antarctica in the south and is bounded by Asia and Australia to the west and the Americas to the east. It contains thousands of islands, often referred to collectively as "Oceania." It has a total population of just under 40 million and is home to one quarter or more (perhaps as many as 2,000) of the earth's approximately 6,000 surviving languages. Of these, approximately one third are classified as "in trouble" or "dying" (Ethnologue, n.d.). As Nettle and Romaine (2000) observe, the parlous state of Pacific languages is due in large part to the impact of European colonization.

If Aotearoa/ New Zealand is excluded, approximately one tenth of the population of the Pacific Islands is now made up of people of European origin. If it is included, the figure is approximately one third. Fishing, agriculture, and tourism play a major role in the economies of most Pacific Islands, with only a few being involved in any significant manufacturing activities. One result of the impact of colonization is that Christianity has tended either to replace traditional beliefs and practices in indigenous societies[1] or to be combined with them. There has, however, been a recent resurgence of traditional belief systems in some areas of the Pacific.

ORIGINS OF THE INDIGENOUS PEOPLES OF THE PACIFIC

The indigenous inhabitants of the Pacific Islands are often collectively referred to as "Pacific Islanders."[2] The Pacific Islands themselves can, however, be divided into three main areas: Melanesia, Polynesia, and

1

Micronesia. The islands that make up Melanesia appear to have been populated by people who emigrated from Africa between 50,000 and 100,000
years ago and who later, probably between 4000 and 3000 BCE, moved
into eastern areas of what is now collectively known as Melanesia. The
islands that make up Polynesia were occupied by people who came from
Southeast Asia in migrations that appear to have begun over 40,000 years
ago, with some of the habitable islands being settled as late as the second
millennium CE. Much less is known about the original inhabitants of the
many small Micronesian islands. It is, however, believed that these islands
were first settled several thousand years ago by people who had previously
settled in Polynesia and Melanesia, the Micronesian cultures combining
aspects of both.

INDIGENOUS PACIFIC CULTURES AND LANGUAGES

Some traditional Pacific Island community cultures have much in common;
others, however, differ in some significant ways. Even so, there *are* some
useful generalizations that can be made so long as it is borne in mind that
there will inevitably be exceptions.

The social structures of Pacific Island communities prior to Western
colonization were traditional in orientation, that is, they were tribal in
nature, having strong kinship bonds and rigidly defined social structures
and expectations. They were characterized by collective ownership, respect
for authority and ancestry, and by custom and ritual. Ceremonial occasions
were often marked by music, dance, and oratory, and historical and practical
knowledge were often embedded in songs, sayings, stories, and legends. A
range of deities, each responsible for some aspect of life or the natural world,
were venerated and often feared in Polynesian and Melanesian societies. A
belief in sorcery and supernatural forces, along with ancestor worship, was,
however, more characteristic of Melanesian communities than it was of
Polynesian ones. For all Pacific communities, the land of their forefathers
had immense spiritual significance. It was, and, for many, remains an animate
life-giving force.

Indigenous Pacific Island languages belong to the Malayo-Polynesian
branch of the Austronesian language family, to the Papuan languages of
New Guinea, or to a mixture of the two. Although many indigenous languages are still spoken throughout the islands, many Pacific Islanders are
no longer able to speak the languages of their ancestors. Most are, however,
familiar with some variety of English or French, one or the other of these
now being an official language *de jure* or *de facto* throughout much of the
Pacific.

COLONIZATION AND RECLAMATION

Oceania was explored by Europeans from the sixteenth century CE onwards. However, major disruption of Pacific social structures did not begin until the late eighteenth century when whalers, traders, and Christian missionaries of various denominations and, finally, waves of settlers, began to make inroads into the Pacific Islands. From the first half of the nineteenth century, as the potential economic and strategic significance of the Pacific became increasingly evident, colonial rule, taking various forms, was established by a number of nations, including Britain, France, Spain, Holland, Germany, Japan, and the United States. Settlers and colonial authorities then began the process of securing land and imposing their own concept of what is appropriate on peoples whom they generally regarded as being linguistically and culturally inferior. In doing so, they used a combination of persuasion and coercion. Indigenous numbers were drastically reduced, in some cases almost to extinction, as a result of introduced ailments, separation from traditional food sources and support networks, and ongoing hostilities. This, combined with the fact that indigenous resistance was often met with a brutal response, meant that the peoples of the Pacific Islands had little recourse but to accept what seemed to be the inevitable loss of their autonomy and traditional lifestyles. As the twentieth century progressed, however, events in other parts of the world, events that often involved civil disobedience and the disruption of previously accepted social and cultural norms, had an impact on Pacific peoples, many of whom began the long and inevitably painful and partial process of reclamation of land, language, and cultural and social identity. For many of those seeking renewed autonomy, there are three very significant documents which support their efforts:

- the *United Nations Declaration on the Granting of Independence to Colonial Countries and Peoples*, adopted on 14 December 1960 by General Assembly Resolution 1514 (XV);
- the *Universal Declaration of Linguistic Rights* (1996, Article 50) (Beatriu Krayenbühl i Gusi: Trans.), adopted at the World Conference on Linguistic Rights in Barcelona;[3] and
- the *United Nations Declaration on the Rights of Indigenous Peoples (2008, p. 6)*.

One extract from each of these documents is printed below:

> [All] peoples have the right to self-determination; by virtue of that right they freely determine their political status and freely pursue their economic, social and cultural development.
>
> *United Nations Declaration on the Granting of Independence to Colonial Countries and Peoples*

[All] language communities have the right for their language to occupy a preeminent place in advertising, signs, external signposting, and in the image of
the country as a whole.
    Universal Declaration of Linguistic Rights

[I]ndigenous peoples and individuals have the right to belong to an indigenous
community or nation, in accordance with the traditions and customs of the community or nation concerned.
    United Nations Declaration on the Rights of Indigenous

THE STUDY OF LINGUISTIC LANDSCAPES

The research reported and discussed in chapters 2 through 6 is centrally
concerned with the concept of "linguistic landscape" (LL), a term that is
relatively recent in research literature, having been introduced by Landry and
Bourhis (1997) to refer to the "visibility and salience of languages on public
and commercial signs in a given territory or region" (p. 23). A sign is now
commonly defined, in line with a definition provided by Backhaus (2007),
as "any piece of text within a spatially definable frame" (p. 66). Research
in the area of LL, however, predates the introduction of the term "linguistic
landscape," as indicated by Backhaus who provides an overview of such
research (pp. 12–39).

It has been argued that landscape is one of the central elements of cultural
systems in that it acts as a signifying system through which social systems
are communicated, reproduced, experienced, and explored (Duncan, 1990, p.
17). Landscape can even be seen as unwitting autobiography (Lewis, 1979, p.
12), that is, as a cultural construct in which our sense of place and memories
inhere (Taylor & Lennon, 2012, p. 1). Thus, "[e]very mature nation has its
symbolic landscapes [which] are part of the iconography of nationhood, part
of the shared idea and memories and feelings which bind people together"
(Meinig, 1979, p. 164). Because landscapes are cultural and creative domains
as well as natural or physical phenomena (Wylie, 2007, p. 8), people may
place themselves in relation to landscapes in creative and imaginative ways,
manifesting their local and/or national sense of self-recognition and social
identity (Stewart & Strathern, 2003, p. 2 & 3).

Central to LL research is what is conveyed, explicitly or implicitly, by
the presence, absence, and/or relative positioning of particular languages
on signs appearing in public spaces (Landry & Bourhis, 1997). Different
languages may convey different messages within the same sign or there may

be semantic duplication, that is, the same message conveyed in different languages (Reh, 2004). However, while the explicit message may appear to be the same in the case of different languages, there may nevertheless be differences in interpretation relating to, for example, the salience of the languages represented, including their positioning and sharpness of focus and the ways in which the signs on which they appear relate to other signs and/or to a particular set of social and historical circumstances (Kress & van Leeuwen, 1988).

Written signs (official; semi-official; sanctioned; unsanctioned) that appear in public spaces remain at the core of LL research. However, LL research now generally extends beyond the analysis of written signage to include, for example, sounds and images analyzed in a wide variety of ways and in relation to a wide range of perspectives in what has been referred to as a "multi-modal approach" (Shohamy & Gorter, 2008). Thus, contemporary LL research may draw upon, and contribute to, an even wider range of disciplines than was the case in more narrowly focused language sign-specific studies in which sociolinguistics, sociology, social psychology, geography, and media studies were prioritized (Sebba, 2010, p. 73). More widely focused LL-centered research may take account not only of the physical context of signage (such as the architectural style of buildings on which the signage appears), but also of people moving into and out of the landscape, their voices contributing to what is now often referred to as the "soundscape."[4,5]

Just as LL is part of landscape more generally, so landscape itself is, in turn, located within an even broader geographical, social, political, and cultural context. In any discussion of LL and its significance, it is, therefore, important to give careful consideration to the context in which it occurs. Jaworski and Thurlow (2010, p. 2), following Scollon and Scollon (2003), use the term "semiotic landscape" to refer to "any [public] space with visible inscription made through deliberate human intervention and meaning making." They prefer this term to "linguistic landscape" in the case of studies in which the emphasis is on the ways in which written discourse interacts with other discursive modalities in public spaces. The primary focus of the studies reported is written language in public spaces, with other discursive modalities providing part of the context for the analysis and discussion of that language. For this reason, the term "linguistic landscape" is retained, the term "semiotoscape" being used to refer to all aspects (including visual and aural) of signification involving intentional human intervention (Johnson, 2017, p. 1). The fact that there is here a primary focus on written language does not entail neglect of other semiotic resources, such as images, sounds, and architecture, which have played a role in other LL-focused studies (see, e.g.,

Barni & Bagna, 2016; Johnson, 2017; Jaworski & Thurlow, 2010; Waksman & Shohamy, 2016).

Each of the studies explored in chapters 2 through 5 begins with an outline of the sociopolitical, geographical, and historical context of the LL under investigation, including aspects of language policy and planning. This is followed by a discussion of the LL itself. That discussion takes account of the wider context in which the LL is situated. This approach is, I believe, consistent with that of Spolsky and Cooper (1991) who, before the term "linguistic landscape" was introduced into the research literature, located a chapter dealing with street signage in a book about the languages of Jerusalem within the context of a richly textured contextual discussion.

Blackwood and Tufi (2015, p. 2) have noted that the city as transactional space presents normative, transgressive, and subversive acts of identity in the context of the interplay of the center and the periphery, the included and the excluded, the fixed and the fluid. This is something that, irrespective of whether the LL in focus is part of a cityscape or, for example, a rural townscape, might be expected to be of particular significance in contexts in which colonized peoples struggle to assert their voices in the face of dominant colonial authorities and ideologies, as is the case in the studies reported here.

There are three main issues in relation to LL research that are of particular relevance so far as the studies reported in this book are concerned. The first is that very little LL research has been conducted in the Pacific region and, in particular, in areas of the Pacific which have been subjected to physical, linguistic, and cultural colonization. The second is that although much of the work in the area of LL to date has been conducted in contexts where there are multilingual and multicultural populations, and although issues of power and resistance are inevitably at the core of LL research (Marten et al., 2012, p. 1), discussion of the ways in which the existing hegemony is supported or challenged by the nature of the LL has not always been theoretically grounded. The third is that LL research has sometimes been said to lack a clear orthodoxy or theoretical core (Sebba, 2010, p. 73). While the last of these is by no means necessarily a problem in itself, it is something that nevertheless indicates the need to be specific in relation to the theoretical underpinning of whatever overall approach is adopted in any particular research project as well as the relationship between that theoretical underpinning and the research methods selected.

Bearing in mind the three issues referred to above, my aim has been to conduct LL research with a Pacific focus, exploring issues relating to colonization and indigeneity from a particular theoretical perspective, that of critical discourse theory (CDT), and associated with CDT, a range of appropriate research methods. Central to CDT is the unmasking and transformation of dominant social structures. This is something that is potentially of major significance in relation to the survival or demise of minority languages whose users have been subjected to one or more types of pressure aimed at persuading or coercing them to abandon these languages in favor of more dominant/ socially acceptable ones (Lewis, 2014, p. 61).

In view of the relationship between LL and identity construction and representation, it is interesting to note that Rubdy and Ben Said (2015, p. 3) provide a number of possible reasons for exclusion of particular languages from the LL. The first of these is the application of top-down policies which assign prestige or stigma to particular languages or language varieties. The second is the result of a sense of insecurity in the face of other dominant ideologies, languages or coercive sociopolitical practices. The third is a lack of coordination between policy and policy implementation. All three of these can be seen to play a role in the studies reported here.

THE RELEVANCE OF CRITICAL DISCOURSE THEORY

The theoretical framework underpinning the studies included in this book is provided by CDT, which centers on the belief that "[m]eanings and identities . . . are radically contingent, [with] antagonistic forces attempting to fix, disrupt and reconfigure them in order to achieve hegemony" (Jørgensen & Phillips, 2002, p. 38). The struggle for hegemony becomes particularly evident where some destabilizing crisis highlights the contingent nature of the *status quo* (Laclau & Mouffe, 1985, pp. 111–113; Torfing, 2005, p. 8),[6] providing a context in which "master signifiers" representing widely accepted ideas (e.g., "democracy") become imbued with new meanings (Jorgensen & Phillips, 2002, pp. 44–45). In such a situation, as Hall and Jefferson (1976) demonstrate, one possible form of resistance is to adopt a "subcultural style," that is, a style that involves reshaping the products and practices of the dominant culture in a way that contributes toward the identity of a particular group, allowing it to win space and mark out an appropriate territory (p. 45). Thus, subcultures may appropriate "certain artefacts and significations from the dominant . . . culture," transforming them "into symbolic forms which take on new meanings and significance" as they shape new identities (Jackson, 1987, p. 9). And because landscape, including LL, is closely allied to identity, it may play an important role in cases where identity is contested and/or reconstituted.

The fact that identity can never be fixed is particularly evident in an increasingly globalized world in which identity formation may involve a struggle to accommodate both the local and the global. In the case of countries that have been subjected to colonization, the impact of globalization can be particularly complex and problematic. While young people of indigenous origin struggle to come to terms with the erosion of their linguistic and cultural heritage, they may nevertheless have global aspirations (Johnson, 2008). Influenced by the media and American popular culture (Melnick & Jackson, 2002, p. 249), they may come to associate the English language with success, wealth, style, and acceptance (Curtin, 2009, p. 229). Meanwhile, their parents may struggle to maintain the language of their forebears and to find ways of maintaining some connection with a past that is a significant part of their identity. Central to LL research is, therefore, of necessity, analysis of the ongoing struggle for hegemony as people seek to fix, contest, or reconfigure meanings and identities, especially at times when some destabilizing crisis highlights their radical contingency. Two examples of this that relate specifically to LL are outlined below.

One example of the impact on the LL of destabilizing crisis is to be found in the recent past of Aotearoa/ New Zealand. On 15 March 2019, during Friday prayers, fifty-one people were killed and forty-nine injured at the Al Noor Mosque and the Linwood Islamic Centre in Christchurch in what has been described as the deadliest killing spree in modern New Zealand history (Watson, 2019). The man accused of the killing is an Australian with links to "white supremacists" around the world. The attack on the Al Noor Mosque was live-streamed on *Facebook*. That attack jolted the people of New Zealand out of a sense of complacency. It met with an immediate and massive response throughout the country. Mosques were inundated with messages of support, floral tributes, and gifts of food. Millions of dollars were donated to support the families of the victims. Vigils were held. Street gangs sent members to mosques around the country to help protect them during prayer times. Māori groups, often joined by non-Māori, performed *haka* (ceremonial war dances) and *waiata* (songs) in honor of the victims. One week after the attack, a Muslim call to prayer was followed by a nation-wide period of silence and an open-air Friday prayer service which was attended by 20,000 people and broadcast nationally on radio and television. Following Prime Minister Jacinda Arden's initiative, many people took up as a mantra: "We are one." The Muslim community was becoming more visible and more confident and it was increasingly being recognized that that community had much in common with other groups, including Māori, whose right to their own way of life was only partially acknowledged and sometimes simply denied.

Throughout all of this time, messages of sympathy were left outside mosques and in other public spaces. Many of these messages were in the Māori language. There were responses indicating thanks, generally in English but sometimes also in Māori and occasionally in other languages. The existing hegemony, with its often unstated racist undercurrent, was being subjected to a major challenge. Changing public attitudes signaling increasing tolerance of difference were in evidence in the LL. This has continued.

Figure 1.1   Sign Outside the Jamia Masjid (Mosque) in Hamilton, New Zealand Shortly after the April 2019 Bombings in Sri Lanka. *Source:* Photo credit Diane Johnson.

Thus, for example, following the April 2019 bombings in Sri Lanka in which many Christian worshipers were killed or injured, the following message, in English and Māori, was posted outside of the Jamia Masjid (mosque) in Hamilton, New Zealand (Waikato district) (see Figure 1 above).

Another example of the impact on the LL of a destabilizing crisis is evident in *The Base*, one of New Zealand's largest retail and commercial *centers* which is built on a block of land that was requisitioned by the New Zealand government prior to World War II and used as an Air Force Base during the war. The land was returned to the Waikato-Tainui Māori tribal confederation in 1995 as part of a package of reparations relating to the Crown's mistreatment of the tribe, including its misappropriation of tribal lands (Johnson, 2017, p. 1). Early responses to the settlement, one of the first between Māori tribes and the Crown, were often flagrantly racist and condescending. One example of this can be seen in the following extract from an editorial that appeared in a New Zealand newspaper six years after the settlement (*New Zealand Herald*, 11 January 2001).

> If Māori tribes are loath to discuss what they have done with Treaty of Waitangi settlements, it is somewhat understandable. They are witnessing the price being paid for failure by Tainui, the settlement trail-blazer. The tribe's financial

performance could hardly be more abject; its wealth has not grown by one dollar since its $170 million settlement in 1995. As its beneficiaries grapple with the dismal outcome of misguided and extravagant investments, Tainui's public humiliation is complete.

Shortly after that editorial was printed, Waikato-Tainui announced its intention to build a retail development on the site of the old Air Force Base. Just twelve years later, tribal assets amounted to more than $1.16 billion (Mana and Money, *Weekend Herald*, 6 February, 2016). Other tribal groups have also made significant gains on the back of financial settlements in spite of the fact that these settlements have been very small indeed in relation to the losses experienced by Māori as a result of colonization. The Base itself is now a successful and sophisticated commercial enterprise. It is also a symbol of resistance and reclamation. In a significant departure from the common practice of including English-only signage in shopping malls in New Zealand, most of the signs for which the owners/ managers of *The Base* as a whole are responsible are bilingual (English and Māori), with a few being in the Māori language only. This, combined with other aspects of *The Base*, including its Tainui-specific architecture, contributes to the re-appropriation of physical and linguistic space.

The Waikato-Tainui settlement and events that followed it represented a destabilizing crisis so far as many New Zealanders were concerned. The radical contingency of the existing hegemony was exposed and contested and master signifiers (Māori and Waikato-Tainui) were imbued with new meanings (Johnson, 2017, p. 21). To place in a New Zealand newspaper an editorial such as the one an extract from which is included above would now be unthinkable.

THE RELATIONSHIP BETWEEN THEORY AND RESEARCH METHODS

As indicated above, underpinning the studies reported here is, in each case, CDT. Associated with CDT is critical discourse analysis (CDA), an approach to the analysis of discourse that is particularly associated with the writings of Norman Fairclough and Ruth Wodak (see, e.g., Fairclough, 1995; Wodak, 2001). Central to CDA is the exploration of the interaction between language and power, and hence, the interaction between language use and social practice. So long as this focus is maintained, a wide range of research methods is potentially compatible with CDA, a guiding principle, however, according to Fairclough (1995), being that consideration should be given not to the analysis of texts in and of themselves, but to the ways in which these texts are produced, distributed and consumed and the sociocultural practices which they exhibit and to which they contribute. In each of the studies reported here, these dimensions of situated linguistic practice are taken into consideration.

In common with many others, including, for example, Stroud (2016), I focus in the analyses not only on the language displayed on signs, but also on other semiotic resources which, in combination with linguistic signage, reinforce or challenge the legitimacy of the established order and underpin issues associated with identity (c.f. Pavlenko & Blackledge, 2004). Where relevant, in common with Pappenhagen et al. (2016), attention is paid to the illocutionary forces of language segments, that is, the actions they perform in context (see Austin, 1960; Searle, 1969). Also, in common with Said and Kasagna (2016), I highlight some of the ways in which intertextuality is brought into play. Included among the semiotic resources explored are language choice and code mixing which, as in the case of parallel text bilingualism in Wales (Coupland, 2010), may contribute to, or be a visible aspect of aspirational identity formation. I also refer on occasion to research conversations with cultural experts and others and, in the case of the New Zealand study, semi-structured interviews. The knowledge and understanding of a range of interviewees and cultural advisers has proved invaluable.

INTRODUCING THE STUDIES

I report here on LL studies conducted in four different Pacific polities which have been subject to colonization: The Hawaiian Kingdom/ Hawaii; Aotearoa/New Zealand; Kanaka/New Caledonia; and Tahiti (part of Te Ao Maohi/ French Polynesia).[7,8] In each case, the languages and cultures of the indigenous peoples have been subjected to a combination of neglect, ridicule, suppression, and exploitation. Indeed, many indigenous languages of the Pacific have been lost altogether and many are on the endangered languages list (Grimes, 1995).

Faced with ongoing encroachment on their lands, languages, cultures, and identities, many indigenous peoples around the Pacific are engaged in struggles that have played out generation after generation, struggles to survive economically, to sustain a way of life that reflects their cultural heritage, to retain or revitalize their languages and to develop or negotiate the hybrid identities that develop with the blending of peoples (Johnson, 2008). Since around the middle of the second half of the twentieth century, these struggles have intensified in the Pacific region, with an increase in activities that signal reclamation and/or reassertion, struggles which, it is argued here, may be reflected, directly or indirectly, in LLs.

In conducting the studies reported here, my primary aim has been to draw attention to the potential of LL research which has a Pacific and post-colonial focus and, in the process, to demonstrate the value of adopting a particular theoretical perspective, that of CDT, central to which is, as indicated above, the ongoing struggle for hegemony as people seek to fix, contest, or reconfigure meanings and identities, especially at times when some destabilizing crisis highlights their radical contingency (Laclau & Mouffe, 1985). In each case, what we encounter, as in a study by Stroud (2016) involving a protest march in South Africa, are LLs being "actively deployed . . . to enhance local engagement, sense of belonging, or acts of resistance, and to create conditions for new emotional geographies of place" (p. 4). As these studies indicate, that struggle does not necessarily result in increased awareness of indigenous peoples' ethical right to at least equal representation in the LL.

The primary focus of The Hawaiian Kingdom/ Hawai'i study is Maunakea, a mountain sacred to Native Hawaiians. In spite of protests by Native Hawaiians and their supporters, a number of observatories have already been built on the mountainside. At the time when the study reported here was conducted, protesters had established a camp on the mountainside in an effort to prevent the building of an additional observatory—a 30-meter telescope approximately 18 storeys high on a 5-acre observatory complex.

Shohamy and Waksman (2012, p. 110) note that "the public space is . . . a dynamic and fluid place, constantly being constructed, deconstructed, and re-constructed." This is particularly evident in the case of protest movements. However, as Said and Kasanga (2006, p. 71) observe, in spite of their mobile and transitory nature in a local sense, protest signs, along with other aspects of the immediate scene of protest, are increasingly attracting global attention. Thus, although, in one sense, protest signs may represent a "transitory linguistic landscape" (Hanauer, 2013, p. 140), they may nevertheless gain a sense of permanency through their availability on a range of media outlets and social media sites (Barni & Bagna, 2016, p. 71). Conceiving of the Internet as space (cyberspace) orients us toward recognition of the way in which those engaging in computer-mediated communication mobilize and re-orient different physical spaces, selecting or filtering out text and images, to create new functional "spaces" (Jones, 2005, 2010). What begin as localized protests representing a reaction to some regional or national issue may achieve global significance through processes of replication and transformation. Equally, the LL of protest may have an immediate impact locally becoming "a powerful means of generating the active participation of passers-by" (Rubdy & Ben Said, 2015, p. 4).

Of particular relevance in the case of the Hawaiian study reported here are articles published in a collection that appeared in the *Journal of Language and Politics* in 2014. These were later published as a book entitled *Occupy: The spatial dynamics of discourse in global protest movements* (Rojo, 2016). Each of these articles focuses on ways in which discourses involving protest and opposition, with their signs, banners, placards, and other communicative genres, even the bodies of the protestors themselves, reconfigure the dynamics of physical spaces, contributing to, drawing upon, and gathering momentum from a wide range of global communicative resources as the local and the global, the physical and the virtual, merge and, in so doing, impact one another. It is from this perspective that Rojo (2014, p. 623) explores the ways in which:

> changes in the conditions of production and circulation of linguistic practices contribute to the "deterritorialization" and "reterritorialization" of space, by means of which protestors replace the traditional organisation and uses of space with their own beliefs, ideologies and communicative practices. . . . [and] the extent to which . . . reterritorialization leads to an in-depth transformation of the forms of communication, which could be, in their turn, not only transforming public spaces, but also social movements themselves, and the way of doing politics.

The protest in focus in the study reported here is located on the side of a mountain rising out of the Pacific Ocean, over 2,000 miles from the mainland of the United States of America, and yet the impact of that protest has arguably been at least as great as the city-based protests reported in *Occupy*.

An interesting aspect of the Maunakea protest is the creativity evident in the composition of some of the signs. As Jones (2010, p. 473) points out:

> When discourse is used creatively it can potentially change the world on two levels; first on the level of the immediate interaction by shifting the relationships of power among participants, creativity reframing the activity that is taking place . . . and second, on the level of society or culture by contesting conventional orders of discourse and opening up possibilities for the imagining of new kinds of social identities and new ways of seeing the world.

It is argued here that the creativity we observe in the semiotoscape of the protest on Maunakea contributes in no small measure to the "temporary recasting of the symbolic and representational meanings at the site of the protest so that they serve the political aims of the demonstrating group" (Hanauer, 2015, p. 208).

In the study conducted in Aotearoa/Zealand, the focus is on signage in the primary commercial area of a small rural township called Tirau which has a population of under 700.[9] The township is built on land that was terraced and farmed by Māori prior to European colonization. Once a thriving rural service center, Tirau was thrown into crisis in the 1990s by a range of government policies, including the removal of agricultural subsidies. This was motivated in large part by Britain's entry into what was then the European Economic Community (EEC) and its consequent withdrawal from trading agreements with its former colony. Tirau survived by gradually re-creating itself as a tourist destination. Of particular relevance so far as this study is concerned is the claim by Jaworski and Thurlow (2010, p. 7) that "our sense of national or regional identity is closely linked to the nation's collective gaze at the physical attributes of the landscape, especially the pictorial, cartographic and textual representation of the countryside." Also of relevance here is the observation by Shohamy and Waksman (2010) that "[c]ontemporary tourism is one of the key domains in which nations construct their discourses of national identity and unity" (p. 23). In discussing signage at the Ha'apala Memorial in Tel Aviv-Jaffa, Shohamy and Waksman note that "[t]he visible hegemony of Hebrew . . . conveys a sense of exclusion," with the positioning of visitors as "outsiders" (p. 251). The creation of a LL that generates a sense of exclusion is something that resonates in the case of the LL of Tirau.

In the context of an examination of the names of stall signs in a Gambian souvenir market, Jaworski and Thurlow (2010) draw attention to the use and adaptation of internationally known commercial names, noting that this is indicative of "discourses on the move." In Tirau, as in the case of Gambia, some of the names of commercial operations are ironically reminiscent of other times and places.

The study conducted in Kanaky/New Caledonia compares the LLs of two different public spaces in Noumea: the *Jean-Marie Tjibaou Cultural Center* and the *Federation of Lay Works* (FOL). The first of these, located on the outskirts of Noumea, is known for its architectural splendor and is officially dedicated to the languages and cultures of the Kanaky people; the second, located in the center of Noumea, is a building, abandoned since 2011, which was once part of a movement whose aim is to promote equal secular educational opportunities in the realms of sport, culture, and peace.

As Markus and Cameron (2002, p. 15) note, "the way buildings are used and the way people using them relate to one another, is largely dependent on the spoken, written and pictorial texts about these buildings." In the case of the *Jean-Marie Tjibaou Cultural Center*, the many discourses extolling its architectural qualities clearly play an important role in relation to responses to the building and its intended function, impacting on the creation of a LL that contrasts in a fundamental way with the LL associated with the *Federation of Lay Works* building which, covered in graffiti, is likely to be seen by many as "disrupt[ing] the aesthetic of authority" (Jaworski & Thurlow, 2010, p. 21), thus signaling some level of "social disquiet" (Pennycook, 2010, p. 144). In connection with this, however, the following observation by Jaworski and Thurlow (2010, p. 22) seems to be particularly pertinent:

> To label all graffiti as "transgressive" or "illegal" is an oversimplification. . . . [In] a situation of conflict, what constitutes a violation of rights for one party, may be an affirming and legitimate reclamation of voice (and space) for another . . . . Graffiti can only be transgressive if one privileges the hegemonic order as the "legitimate" order.

The Tahitian study focuses on the signage, including street names, in a central area of the capital city, Pape'ete, where approximately half of the entire population of Te Ao Mā'ohi/French Polynesia now live. Of particular significance here is the following observation by Pappenhagen, Scarvaglieri, and Redder (2016, p. 152):

> Names tell stories of origin and belonging, even before any process of mutual communication is to be conducted. . . . [providing] elements of knowledge that are necessary for people to be something to each other . . . [contributing] to the construction of group-related identities. . . . [and serving] to anchor places in the biographical history of their . . . owners . . . [rendering] these places distinguishable from other places . . . and [contributing] to the construction of unique, recognizable societal space.

In the streets of Pape'ete, we are constantly reminded that "[t]he social construction of space is one of the main elements of imperialism" (Jacobs, 1996, p. 158). Here, it is impossible to escape the relevance of Ingles' observation about the relationship between landscape and history:

> A landscape is the most solid appearance in which a history can declare itself. . . .There it is, the past in the present, constantly changing and renewing itself, as the present rewrites the past (Inglis, 1977, p. 489).

Of particular relevance so far as the study conducted in Pape'ete ete is concerned is Kuhn's (2011, p. 45) reminder that "modern ideas about city planning and architecture [have been] used to demonstrate . . . the authority of the state" (Kuhn, 2011, p. 45).

Overall, although each of these studies was conducted in a different polity and in a different local context, all of them are concerned with issues relating to indigeneity, exploitation, and loss. Each demonstrates how the display of a language or of languages in public spaces may represent a political act of inclusion, exclusion and/or deletion (Barni & Bagna, 2016, p. 56).

NOTES

1. The use of the word "indigenous" has proved to be contentious in recent years for good reason. I use it here, however, simply to refer to the descendants of those who occupied the Pacific Islands in waves of settlement prior to Western colonization. I use the term "native," however, when referring to people of Hawaiian ancestry because this is a term they generally prefer.

2. Māori people of Aotearoa/ New Zealand sometimes refer to Pacific Islands peoples *other than themselves* as "Pacific Islanders."

3. This document was presented to the Director General of UNESCO in 1996 but has not been formally approved by UNESCO.

4. For a discussion of soundscape within the context of landscape, see Backhaus (2015).

5. The concept of "soundscape," defined by Schafer (1977, p. 7) as "any acoustic field of study," was applied to spoken language in public spaces by Scarvaglieri et al. (2013) and has since been applied in the context of LL by others, including, for example, Pappenhagen et al. (2016).

6. This type of event can be compared with the concept of "turbulence" as outlined by Cresswell and Martin (2012, p. 516). This concept of turbulence has been applied with reference to the semiotics of citizenship within the context of LL-based research .by Stroud (2016).

7. "Kanaka" is a Polynesian word meaning "human." It originally referred exclusively to Hawaiians but was later used to refer more generally to workers from the Pacific Islands. Although it tends now to be avoided in some parts of the world, including Australia, being regarded as offensive, it has been reclaimed by the indigenous people of New Caledonia and is now widely used by them.

8. I use here English names with reference to the areas of investigation, preceded, where possible, by names often preferred by the indigenous people of these areas. In subsequent chapters, after an initial use of both terms, I revert to the term most widely used.

9. Among those who have investigated small town or rural linguistic landscapes are Bhatia (2000), whose focus is on advertising in rural India, and Thistlethwaite and Sebba (2015), who explore the use of Irish in the "private" linguistic landscape.

Introduction to Part I

BRITAIN AND THE UNITED STATES

COLONIALISM AND EXPANSIONISM

BRITAIN

In common with other European powers, Britain's aim in occupying overseas territories was a combination of prestige, power, control, economic exploitation, strategic political positioning, and in some cases, particularly after its population explosion in the nineteenth century, the provision of locations for settler development. Existing peoples were generally deprived of much of their land and their economic and political power and control. Their cultural and linguistic heritage was treated as inferior, with assimilation to British beliefs and practices being assumed to be in their best interests (Wolfe, 2006).

In the fifteenth and sixteenth centuries, Britain's colonial focus was on the Americas and Asia. The seventeenth century saw its settlement of North America and some smaller Caribbean islands. Although there were major colonial losses associated with the American War of Independence (1783), victory in the Revolutionary and Napoleonic Wars (1792–1815) left Britain largely unchallenged as an imperial power so that by the middle of the nineteenth century it had control over most of India. Also by the nineteenth century, it had expanded into Egypt, South Africa, Australia, and New Zealand. At its height, the British Empire, made up of a range of colonies, protectorates, mandates, and other territories, was the largest empire in history, with over 400 million people and covering over 35 million km². By the beginning of the twentieth century, however, Britain's economic power had begun to be challenged and by the end of World War II, it could no longer exercise control over vast overseas territories. The colonial enterprise was no longer viable. It was at this point (in 1949) that a number of former colonies joined with Britain to form the Commonwealth of Nations, a group of independent states, some of which shared a single (British) monarch.

THE UNITED STATES OF AMERICA

Following the gaining of its independence, the United States of America under President George Washington adopted a policy of non-interventionism. The *Monroe Doctrine of 1821* opposed European colonialism and included an undertaking not to interfere in existing European colonies. In 1846, however, the *Mexican-American War* ended with the annexation by the United States of 1,359,743 km² of Mexican territory. With the *Spanish-American War*, the United States abandoned any pretence of non-interventionism. When Spain withdrew from Cuba in 1898, Cuba was subjected to U.S. military rule until it gained its independence in 1902. After the war, Spain ceded its Pacific possessions, Puerto Rico, the Philippines and Guam, to the United States for US $20 million under the terms of the *Treaty of Paris* (1898). Following the *Philippine-American War* (1899–1902), which arose out of Philippine resistance to U.S. control, the United States created a Philippine Assembly (Philippine Organic Act 1902) and, later, declared its commitment to the eventual granting of independence to the Philippines (*Jones Act/ Philippine Autonomy Act* 1916), with independence finally being granted in 1946 (*Treaty of Manilla*).

Following World War I, the United States returned to its initial non-interventionist stance so far as colonial possessions were concerned, presenting itself as the defender of democracy. Even so, it overthrew Iran's democratically elected government in 1953 and has subsequently become involved in a range of conflicts which appear to have been motivated at least as much by its own economic and/or strategic interests as by altruism. In addition, while being an outspoken advocate for European decolonization after World War II, the United States retains as territories the wartime acquisitions of Guam, Puerto Rico, the U.S. Virgin Islands, American Samoa, and the Northern Mariana Islands. The Marshall Islands, the Federated States of Micronesia, and Palau became freely associated states acting as military bases in exchange for participation in U.S. federal government programs (Immerwahr, 2019). In the case of Hawai'i, following illegal military occupation and fraudulent annexation at the beginning of the twentieth century, a referendum was held in which its residents, then largely of U.S. origin, were offered the option of its becoming a U.S. state. Meanwhile, Native Americans were being subjected to land alienation and social and cultural discrimination. It was not until 1924 that U.S. citizenship was granted to all Native American citizens, with some states continuing to deny them voting rights for several decades.

Chapter 2

The Hawaiian Kingdom: Mount Maunakea

Assertion, Resistance, and the Mise en Abyme *Effect*

A BRIEF HISTORY OF THE HAWAIIAN ISLANDS AND ITS PEOPLE

Location and First Settlements

The isolated Hawaiian archipelago, stretching almost 2,400 km in length, is the northernmost archipelago in Polynesia, located approximately 3,200 km southwest of the United States of America. It is made up of many islands, islets and atolls, including eight main volcanic islands: *O'ahu, Maui, Kaua'i, Moloka'i, Lāna'i, Ni'ihau* and *Kaho'olawe*, and *Hawai'i* (also known as *Hawai'i Island* or *Big Island* to distinguish it from the island group as a whole).[1] The climate is largely tropical but can vary from tropical through temperate to alpine on the slopes. In different locations on the same island it may be dry (less than 510 mm of rain annually) or wet (more than 5,100 mm).

The first settlers arrived no later than 800 CE, possibly as early as 300, with arrivals continuing until around 1300. These settlers appear to have been largely from, initially, the Marquesas, followed by peoples from other areas of Polynesia, including Tahiti. Collectively known as *Kānaka Maoli*, they established a caste-based society, with settlements ruled by *ali'i* (local chiefs). The language which evolved, *ka 'ōlelo Hawai'i*, has been classified as belonging to the Proto-Marquesic group of eastern Polynesian languages (Green, 1966).

It is possible that Spanish explorers were the first Europeans to discover the islands in the sixteenth century CE. What is certain is that the British explorer, Captain James Cook, landed on the islands in 1778 and again in 1779 (when he was killed on the island of Hawai'i following a dispute). The islands were subsequently visited by explorers, traders, and whalers whose presence resulted in the introduction of diseases such as smallpox, influenza, and measles. The arrival of Chinese immigrants in the late eighteenth century is said to have been the likely source of leprosy, which had a devastating impact on the local population, resulting in the establishment of a leper colony on Moloka'i in 1866. As a result of introduced diseases and loss of traditional resources and support networks, the first settler population fell from what may have been around 300,000 in the 1770s to 24,000 in 1920.

Establishment of the Hawaiian Kingdom

The year 1795 marked the end of a series of battles which resulted in the unification of six of the eight main islands, with the remaining two (Kaua'i and Ni'ihau) joining them voluntarily fifteen years later. The ruler, King Kamehameha (later known as King Kamehameha I), established a dynasty (the Kamehameha dynasty) that lasted until 1872. During his reign, the export of sandalwood to China represented the beginning of international trading links, with the United States becoming the chief trading partner. By the time King Kamehameha I died in 1819, the Kingdom had a thriving army and navy.

During the reign of King Kamehameha II, many members of the community converted to Christianity, with Protestant missionaries becoming extremely powerful. This led in 1840 to the signing by King Kamehameha III of a Constitution which stated that the government was based on Christian values. Fearing foreign encroachment on the Kingdom's territory, however, King Kamehameha III dispatched a delegation to the United States and Europe in 1842 to secure assurance of recognition of the Kingdom's independence. That assurance was provided by the United States, France, and Britain.[2] In 1846, the king agreed to transfer Hawaiian land from common to private ownership. This was largely to protect the land from any attempt to secure it by a foreign power in the future. Two years later, the land was divided among the king, chiefs, and commoners. The king's share of the common lands was then divided into Government lands and Crown lands. In 1856, during the reign of King Kamehameha IV, it was determined by statute that Crown lands should be managed in a way that would provide an income for future monarchs. However, as the number of Native Hawaiians decreased and the survival of the people as a whole became increasingly uncertain, Crown Lands became a resource to support both the monarchy and the Native Hawaiian people.

The fifth monarch, King Kamehameha V, reigned from 1830 until 1872. During his reign, a new, more democratic, constitution was enacted and many traditional practices were revived, including the recognition of *kāhuna*, that is, people given special respect for their skills in a range of disciplines including agriculture, canoe building, navigation, healing, and sorcery (Kupihea, 2001; McBride, 2000). Following the death without heir of King Kamehameha V, King Lunalilo was elected, ushering in a second dynasty, that of the House of Kalākaua. When King Lunalilo died a year later, also without heir, King Kalākaua was elected (1874). He was forced by non-Hawaiian residents, who were supported by soldiers and armed militia, to agree to a new constitution (often referred to as the *Bayonet Constitution*, 1887) which removed most of the monarch's authority and denied voting rights to Asians, giving such rights only to those Hawaiian, American, and European males (including residents) who were able to meet economic and literacy requirements.

Overthrow of the Hawaiian Kingdom

King Kalākaua was succeeded in 1891 by his sister, Queen Lili'uokalani, who came to the throne during a period of economic crisis brought about in part by the ending of an agreement which provided Hawaiian exporters with advantages in relation to trade with the United States.[3] In the year of her succession, Queen Lili'uokalani determined that sections of Crown Land would be subdivided into 10 acre plots provided on a thirty-year lease at a nominal yearly rent, her wish being that it would be mainly Native Hawaiians who would benefit.

Following Queen Lili'uokalani's announcement of plans to form a new constitution, one which would restore power to the monarchy and give voting rights to those who had been disenfranchised on economic grounds, a group of European and American business residents and politicians (referred to as the *Committee of Safety*) staged a coup (January 17, 1893) and established a provisional government, the eventual goal being the overthrow of the monarchy and annexation by the United States. In response to claims that there was an imminent threat to U.S. lives and property, U.S. Minister John Stevens arranged for a group of U.S. sailors and Marines to be made available to protect members of the Committee. The administration of the provincial government then commissioned the U.S. government to produce a report about the circumstances leading to the current situation. That report (*the Blount Report*, 1893), produced during the term of President Grover Cleveland, concluded that the removal of Queen Lili'uokalani had been illegal and demanded that she be reinstated. When the Provisional Government refused, the U.S. Congress issued a further report (*the Morgan Report*, 1894). This time, the conclusion was that the coup was necessary in view of the queen's announced intention to redraw the constitution.

In 1894, the royalist faction in The Hawaiian Kingdom began to secretly amass an army and in the following year they attempted to take back power. Queen Lili'uokalani was arrested when a weapons cache was found on the palace grounds. She was tried by a military tribunal, convicted of treason, and placed under house arrest in her own home, the 'Iolani Palace. On January 24, 1895, while under house arrest, she was forced to sign a five-page declaration (*Lili'uokalani Dominis*) in which she formally abdicated in return for the release of her jailed supporters. In that same year, the illegally constituted government amalgamated Government and Crown Lands, depriving the queen of any source of income.

After his election as U.S. President in 1896, Willian McKinley gave way to pressure and agreed to a treaty of annexation. Although that treaty was never ratified by the U.S. Senate, an annexation Resolution (*the Newlands Resolution*) was passed by the House and subsequently by the Senate. In 1900, the United States declared the islands to be a territory of the United States.

By 1896, 57 percent of all taxable land was controlled by residents of European or American ancestry. In 1898, however, a joint resolution of the U.S. Congress determined that revenues from "Public Lands" be retained in a fund intended to provide educational and other benefits to Native Hawaiians. In 1921, just over 200,000 acres that had been part of Crown and Government Land were set aside under the terms of the *Hawaiian Homes Commission Act* to provide independent livelihood (homesteads) for the Native Hawaiian population which was in serious decline. The Hawaiian blood quantum eligibility for receiving homestead land was, however, set at a level that rendered many ineligible and the productive land was, in any case, largely retained in settler hands. Although Native Hawaiians gained little in a practical sense from this exercise, it did represent an implicit acknowledgment of the fact that Crown Lands were lands that had been held by Hawaiian monarchs in trust for the Native Hawaiian people and, by implication, that agreements entered into by Hawaiian monarchs continued to have at least some validity.

In the 1950s, Hawaiian residents who were keen to gain representation in Congress campaigned for statehood. In March 1959, Congress passed the *Hawaii Admission Act* and in June of that year held a referendum asking residents to vote on whether to become a U.S. state or to remain a U.S. territory. The option of voting for the restoration of independence was not available. The vast majority of voters opted for statehood. In 1993, however, the U.S. Congress passed a resolution of apology signed by President Clinton. That resolution acknowledged that the overthrow of the Hawaiian kingdom had been illegal and had taken place with the active participation of agents and citizens of the United States. It further acknowledged that the Native Hawaiian people had never directly relinquished to the United States their claims to their inherent sovereignty as a people over their national lands.

The Hawaiian Islands as a U.S. Military Base

In 1898, three years after the forced abdication of Queen Lili'uokalani, the United States declared war on Spain, seeking to capture its overseas territories in the Pacific and using the Hawaiian Islands as a military base from which to launch attacks against Guam and the Philippines. This was the beginning of what was to become ongoing use of the islands for military purposes and it was this that ultimately led to the Japanese attack on Pearl Harbor in Honolulu on the island of O'ahu in December 1941, an attack which brought the United States into World War II.

Currently, Hawai'i has the largest concentration of U.S. military bases (11), with approximately 50,000 military personnel assigned there. On Kaho'olawe, which was used as a training ground and bombing range during World War II, live training exercises did not cease until 1990. In 1994, the island was returned to the State of Hawai'i. Although the U.S. navy was retained to develop and implement a clearance and restoration project, not all hazardous materials were removed and the island continues to be unsafe.

The Indigenous People: Culture and Language

Traditional Hawaiian religion is polytheistic and animistic, with the physical and non-physical realms being intermingled, and with warnings, omens, and protection being provided by deities, spirits, and guardians. Day-to-day interactions are subject to a system of taboos, designed to protect the pure from the impure. All aspects of life, including canoe-making, fishing, and food preparation, require an attitude of respect and thankfulness. Reconciliation and forgiveness, as in many areas of the southern Pacific, are central aspects of the culture. One of the best known dances, the Hula (*Ha'a*), which was banned for many years, is a complex and subtle art form in which movements of the body represent feelings, emotions, and natural phenomena, such as the swaying of trees in the breeze. There are now two main branches of Hula—*Hula Kahiko*, which is accompanied by chanting and the playing of traditional instruments, and *Hula Auana*, which is accompanied by introduced musical instruments, such as the guitar or 'ukulele.

The Hawaiian language (*ōlelo Hawai'i*) first appeared in written form in the early nineteenth century in a version of the Latin alphabet developed by an American Protestant missionary.[4] Within a few decades, the vast majority of Native Hawaiians could read and write and Hawaiian newspapers flourished, as did Hawaiian-medium schools. Well into the early decades of the twentieth century, Native Hawaiians continued to speak the Hawaiian language (although they also learned English at school) and many settlers spoke the language in addition to their mother tongue. However, stigmatization of Hawaiian language and culture, together with educational policies that prioritized English, led to a situation in which there were probably fewer than 1,000 native speakers by the last decade of the twentieth century.

In 1846, the legislature of the Kingdom of Hawai'i had announced that all laws enacted were to be published in both *ōlelo Hawai'i* and English. By 1850, however, English had become the dominant language in most public domains, including that of government. Even so, until 1943, laws continued to be published in both languages. In 1943, however, the practice of publishing laws *in ōlelo Hawai'i* was abolished by statute (Walk, 2008, sec. II, paras. 4 & 5).

The first government-sponsored school conducted through the medium of English was established in 1851. From that point on, Hawaiian-medium schools were constantly undermined until, finally, all were closed. An early attempt at "official" suppression of the Hawaiian language is to be found in the 1905 *Revised School Laws* (p. 8):

> The English Language shall be the medium and basis of instruction in all public and private schools, PROVIDED, that where it is desired that another language shall be taught in addition to the English language, such instruction may be authorized by the department, either by its rules, the curriculum of the school, or by direct order in any particular instance. Any schools that shall not conform to the provisions of this section shall not be recognized by the Department.

It was not long, however, before *ōlelo Hawai'i* no longer need be seen as a threat. Thus, the School Laws for 1922 were amended to read:

> provided, however, that the Hawaiian language shall be taught in addition to the English at all normal and high schools of the Territory.

Schütz (1994, p. 359) comments on this as follows:

> The legislature's plans . . . were—at best—farcical, and—at worst—insulting to the language and culture, for they proposed to teach the language with an embarrassingly inadequate text, no trained teachers, and no program with which to train them.

The situation, however, arguably worsened. The 1962 version of the School Laws (pp. 28–29) directed as follows:

> Daily instruction for at least ten minutes in conversation or, in [*sic*] the discretion of the department, in reading and writing, in the Hawaiian language shall be given in every public school conducted in any settlement of homesteaders under the Hawaiian homes commission.

The 1966 version of the School Laws makes no mention at all of the Hawaiian language (Schütz, 1994, p. 359). Even so, in the 1960s and 1970s, the beginning of a Hawaiian renaissance movement was under way and could not be ignored for long. Thus, in 1978, *ka ōlelo Hawai'i* was recognized as one of the official languages of the State of Hawai'i. Declaring a language to be "official" is, however, little more than tokenism unless that declaration is accompanied by a clear statement of what "official" actually means in practice. Although it seems that the official status of *ka 'ōlelo Hawai'i* was not intended to have any significant impact on day-to-day life, the introduction of the Native American Languages Act (1990)[5] provided a potential opportunity to change that. That Act affirms the right of "Native Americans" to express themselves through the use of their heritage languages, a right not to be restricted in any public proceeding. Even so, in 2017, the House of Representatives of the State of Hawai'i insisted that it was not obliged to make documentation available in the Hawaiian language.[6]

It is now almost exclusively on the privately owned Ni'ihau Island, which has restricted access to non-residents, that native speakers of the language who use it on a day-to-day basis are to be found.[7,8] According to a 2010 census, the population of Ni'ihau, which has no telephone services, no paved roads, no power lines, and no running water, was 170.[9] The Ni'ihau dialect, which is believed to be closer to the language spoken prior to European contact, differs in a number of ways from what is now sometimes referred to as "standard Hawaiian."

Although the number of native speakers of the Hawaiian language is now very limited, a significant number of Hawaiians have learned Hawaiian as a second language and some are now passing the language on to their children. There are also Hawaiian immersion schools and pre-schools throughout Hawai'i and Hawaiian language courses are thriving in tertiary institutions.[10]

So far as the courts are concerned, however, there has, until very recently, appeared to be an absolute determination to avoid recognizing the Hawaiian language as having any role to play. In 1993, William Tagupa, a Hawaiian attorney, brought an employment discrimination suit against the University of Hawai'i, attempting to give his deposition in the Hawaiian language (Kupau, 2004). The judge required that he respond in English. In response to Tagupa's appeal against that decision, a federal judge ruled that, in view of the fact that Tagupa spoke both the English and Hawaiian languages, it would be an unnecessary expense to hire an interpreter and would, in addition, needlessly delay the deposition. In January 2018, Samuel Kaleikoa Ka'eoa,[11] accused of petty misdemeanors in relation to protest action concerning the construction of a 30-meter telescope (see below for further details on related protest action), refused to identify himself in English in court, instead indicating in the Hawaiian language that he was present (*eia no wau ke ku nei*). The judge responded with "I don't know what that means" (Rivas, 25 Jan 2018) and issued a warrant for his arrest (Wang, March 1, 2018). The prosecution's argument was a now familiar one: compelling the court to hire an interpreter would be impractical and an unnecessary expense bearing in mind the fact that Ka'eoa could speak English (Hiraishi, Jan 24, 2018).

EXPLORING THE LINGUISTIC LANDSCAPE

Introducing the Primary Site of Protest

The Hawaiian Islands are made up of a chain of volcanic mountains. These volcanic mountains give the land and its people their distinctive character, contributing to their history, their lore, and their fascination. They also help to sustain the delicate balance of one of the most biologically diverse regions in the world, a region which, however, now has the highest rate of species extinctions on earth. One of these mountains was the location of the study reported here. The name of that mountain, located on the Big Island, is generally represented as *Mauna Kia, Mauna Kea,* or *Maunakea*. These are often translated as "White Mountain." In fact, however, the word for "white" in the Hawaiian language is "kea" (not "kia") and so the first orthographic representation of the name of the mountain, although it appears in some "official" contexts, is simply wrong. In any case, the representation that is preferred by many Native Hawaiians is *Maunakea*. This is considered by many Native Hawaiians to be a shortened version of *Mauna a Wākea*, the mountain of Wākea, one of the legendary ancestors of the Hawaiian people. Maunakea's peak, over 4,000 feet above sea level, marks the highest point of the Hawaiian Islands and is, when measured from its oceanic base, the tallest mountain in the world. For native Hawaiians, *Maunakea* is, unsurprisingly, one of the most sacred places on earth. It is also one of the best sites in the world for astronomical observation.

In the early 1960s, very shortly after Hawai'i had been declared the fiftieth State of the United States of America, the Hawaiian Chamber of Commerce promoted astronomical development on Maunakea. This was in spite of the fact that it is Crown Land. In 1964, an access road was built and thirteen enormous observation facilities funded by eleven countries were located at what is referred to as the *Mauna Kea Science Reserve*. In 2013, plans to build the largest and most powerful facility of all were approved. These plans related to the building, on a five-acre complex, of a 30-meter telescope (TMT) approximately 18 stories high at a cost of US$1.4 billion. In October 2014, a ceremony which was intended to celebrate this proposed development was interrupted by protesters. Since then, protest has continued. On April 2,

2015, when around 300 protesters gathered near the visitors' center, 12 were arrested. A further eleven were arrested near the summit of the mountain. When protest expanded beyond the mountain, construction was halted temporarily (April 7, 2015). On October 31, 2018, however, the Supreme Court of Hawai'i ruled that construction could go ahead. It was scheduled to begin on July 15, 2019. On July 13, protesters blocked the access road to the summit of the mountain, denying passage to construction traffic. As in the case of previous protests about the telescopes, this was a peaceful protest. Even so, during the first week of the protest action, several Native Hawaiian elders were arrested. Protest continued, arrests continued. Protest spread from the mountain to other parts of Hawai'i, to the United States and, very rapidly, to many sites throughout the world.

On August 11, 2011, astronomer Tom Kerr wrote in a post relating to the protest: "It seems to me that it's an argument about returning to the stone age versus understanding our universe" (Kerr, 2011, August 18). More recently, in April 2015, a professor at the University of California Berkley sent a link to a petition in support of the TMT which contained a note from a professor at the University of California Santa Cruz claiming that "the Thirty-Meter Telescope is in trouble, attacked by a horde of native Hawaiians who are lying about the impact of the project on the mountain and who are threatening the safety of TMT personnel" (Solomon, 2015). There was an immediate response from scientists around the world who found the comment offensive. As Herman (2015) observed:

What is really at stake . . . is a conflict between two ways of knowing and being in the world. For many Native Hawaiians and other Indigenous peoples, sacredness is not merely a concept or label. It is a lived experience of oneness and connectedness with the natural and spiritual worlds. It is as common sense as believing in gravity. This experience is very much at odds with the everyday secular-humanist approach of Western thinking . . . which sees no "magic" or "enchantment" in the world. And of course, seeing nature as inert facilitates both commercial exploitation and scientific exploration.

In a memorandum dated February 25, 2018, Dr. de Zayas[12] concluded that the Hawaiian Islands were under a strange form of occupation by the United States, having been illegally occupied and fraudulently annexed. Dr. de Zayas had recently reviewed a complaint submitted in 2017 to the United Nations Office of the High Commissioner for Human Rights in which the complainant[13] had referenced the historical and ongoing plundering of the Hawaiians' lands, drawing attention, in particular, to the plundering of lands whose rightful heirs and descendants had land titles that originated from the distributions of lands under the authority of The Hawaiian Kingdom. In relation to this, Dr. de Zayas concluded that "[t]he State of Hawai'i courts should not lend themselves to flagrant violation of the rights of the land title holders [and] . . . must not enable or collude in the wrongful taking of private lands."

The Changing Linguistic Landscape of Maunakea: Reviewing Six Weeks from July 13, 2019

From July 13, 2019, large numbers of signs began to appear on the mountainside, some displayed by "State authorities," others by protesters. The linguistic landscape of the mountainside was changing from day to day and sometimes from hour to hour. Although this made any attempt at accurate statistical analysis impossible, it *is* possible to make some general quantitative observations about the signs for which protesters were responsible. In the early days of the 2019 protest, the majority of the signs on the mountainside (banners, placards, etc.) were in the Hawaiian language. In the case of signs identifying facilities provided by the protesters (e.g., medical tent and school), they continued to be in Hawaiian or, occasionally, in a mixture of the Hawaiian and English languages. Signs in English began to proliferate, however, when the protest began to attract widespread national and international attention. Overall, in the first six weeks of the 2019 protest (the period covered here), approximately one third of protesters' signs were in the Hawaiian language or in a combination of English and Hawaiian.

As news of the protest spread, pictures of signs, banners and placards that had appeared on the mountain began also to appear, along with some of the words of the protesters and commentary about the protest, in local and international media and in social media outlets. This created something similar to a *mise en abyme* effect,[14] with constantly repeated photographs, copies, and adaptations of the signs appearing in physical and virtual locations throughout the world in such a way as to suggest an infinitely recurring sequence.

Figure 2.1 below shows one of the first large protest banners to appear on the mountainside alongside a range of placards. The banner reads ROAD CLOSED DUE TO DESECRATION, the first four words echoing the type of official informational/ instructional road signage that is commonly used to prevent traffic from entering a particular zone. Although these words are generally associated with official notification, they are followed here not, for example, by a word that makes reference to the result of some natural phenomenon (e.g., subsidence) but, rather, by a word that refers to a type of disrespectful, sacrilegious human intervention (i.e., desecration). The result is a banner that acts as an assertion or reminder (depending on the reader's perspective) of the sacred nature of the mountain. The effect of

Figure 2.1 Protesters on Mount Maunakea with a Banner Referring to Desecration.
Source: Photo Credit AP Images/Caleb Jones.

this entextualization is to suggest that the protesters have both the official and the moral authority, with those who might *appear* to be the authority figures being nothing more than trespassers and vandals. This implicature is reinforced by an image at the top of the banner which takes the form of two crossed sticks with a ball of tapa cloth at the top of each. Cross pieces of this type (*pūlo'ulo'u*) are used at the entrance to traditional Hawaiian temple sites (*heiau*) as a warning that these sites are sacred and that commoners should not enter.[15] Thus, the protesters/protectors are presented as guardians while the "authorities" are presented as upstarts/trespassers who would violate the sanctity of a sacred place. And all of this is conveyed, at least to those who understand some of the historical and cultural issues involved, in just five words. Hardly surprising, therefore, that this banner has been produced and reproduced over and over again on physical and virtual sites around the world, becoming an icon of indigenous resistance.

There is another widely circulated photograph (not reproduced here) in which the same banner appears. In that photograph, the Hawaiian flag can be seen flying above the banner. That flag, designed at the request of Kamehameha, has eight stripes, each one representing one of the eight main islands of the Hawaiian Kingdom. Positioned as it is, high over the heads of the protesters, it is reminiscent of a battle ensign. However, because it is flying upside-down (an international symbol of a person or nation in distress), it further symbolizes the gathering together in battle formation of a distressed nation. In the corner of the Hawaiian flag is an image of the British flag. That image was included initially as a signal of The Hawaiian Kingdom's historical relations with Britain. Now, however, it serves as reminder of the fact that Britain's official recognition of The Hawaiian Kingdom did not translate into effective opposition to the illegal takeover by the United States.

Also visible in that photograph are four placards reading WE ARE HERE TO PROTECT MAUNAKEA. The duplication of what had first appeared as a single protest sign reinforces the impact of the inclusive pronoun. At the center of each of these placards is an image of the mountain from which white birds are ascending. These high flying, gliding birds, white tailed *koa'e*, are considered by Native Hawaiians to be guardians or lookouts and are currently the subject of a conservation plan, their survival as a species being of high concern. Their inclusion, therefore, acts not only as a reinforcement of the concept of watchfulness and guardianship, but also as a reminder that the desecration of the mountain extends beyond the mountain itself and includes a threat to the flora and fauna over which Native Hawaiians have traditionally exercised stewardship.

A further sign in that photograph, one that also includes a picture of the mountain, reads CROWN LANDS in English and underneath, in the Hawaiian language, *KŪ KIA'I MAUNA* (STANDING GUARD OVER THE MOUNTAIN). This is a reminder for those with some understanding of Hawaiian history of the significance of Crown Lands to Native Hawaiians. The loss of these lands has been fundamental to the severing of the Native Hawaiian ties to the land, including the sacred mountains, and, hence, to their sense of alienation and betrayal. The use of the Hawaiian language in that sign impacts in a number of different ways. It serves as an assertion of linguistic rights, as a symbol of inclusion and community in the case of shared Native Hawaiian identity, and, potentially, as a motivator or aspirational target for those Native Hawaiians who do not speak the language of their ancestors.

Just visible to the left of the picture under discussion is an "official" road sign in green reading MAUNA KEA ACCESS with a red stop sign underneath. The stop sign was added by the protesters. Something that is of particular interest so far as that "official" road sign is concerned is the fact that the mountain's name is written as two words rather than one. The "official" preference for MAUNA KEA (translated as *White Mountain*) rather than MAUNAKEA (generally translated by Native Hawaiians as *Mountain of Wākea*) is, however, what might be expected in a context in which any apparent reference to a legendary progenitor of Native Hawaiian people might act as a reminder of indigenous rights to the land. Equally, it may simply be that those responsible for road signage have no knowledge or understanding of the representational subtleties of Hawaiian place names.

Most of the signs so far discussed are in English and, therefore, appear to be addressed not only to Native Hawaiians, but also to those living in Hawaiʻi who are not native to the islands, to U.S. citizens more generally and to the world at large. Even so, the images that accompany the words, particularly the *pūloʻuloʻu* (crossed sticks) and white tailed *koaʻe,* have particular significance for Native Hawaiians, drawing them into a community of understanding which is also a community of common heritage and shared loss in relation to which others are outsiders.

Also significant so far as the impact of many of the signs captured in photographs and distributed around the world are concerned is their positioning, clustered together with the haunting mountain landscape. Although that landscape changes with the weather and the time of day, one thing that is always in evidence is the grandeur of the mountain views.

The Maunakea observatory protest has never been solely about the proposed building of a further telescope on the mountain. That proposal, offensive though it is in itself to many Native Hawaiians, has provided a focus for a more general protest—a protest against the illegal occupation of The Hawaiian Kingdom by the United States. It is this, in particular, that Native Hawaiians want U.S. citizens and, indeed, citizens of the world more generally, to be made aware of. It is this, along with the desecration of their lands, for which they seek redress. Hence, signs such as the one below that appeared alongside the protest camp soon after the beginning of the 2019 protest (see Figure 2.2).

The placard in Figure 2.2 acts as a reminder of the illegal occupation by the United States of The Hawaiian Kingdom. It also, for those who are aware of the islands' history, acts as a reminder of the fact that that Kingdom was officially recognized by European nations, as well as the United States, prior to that occupation. For those who are *not* aware of the islands' history, a placard such as this can potentially serve as an educational tool. Indeed, that is precisely the role it has served for some of those who have visited the protest camp, the camp thus performing an educational function as well as an oppositional one.

The protesters' base camp includes all sorts of facilities:

There is a tented cafeteria providing free meals, and a community-run medic station, daycare and school. Along the barren roadside, tropical flowers have been casually stuck in traffic cones. People pound taro, a Hawaiian crop, in the traditional way on wooden boards to make poi, a local dish. (Van Dyke, 2019)

The educational function that is evident in the placard in Figure 2.2 has by no means been confined to the immediate site of the protest. Thus, for example, an article by Maile Arvin[16] (2019, July 27) appeared in *Truthout* shortly after

Figure 2.2   A Placard That Appeared Alongside the Maunakea Protest Camp. *Source:* Photo Credit Steven Chase.

the beginning of the 2019 protest. It was accompanied by a photograph of the sign in Figure 2.2 and had the following headline:

Mauna Kea Protests are Part of a Long Fight Against Colonialism

In what appears to be a clear attempt to reinforce state power and control, the Hawaiian *State Department of Transportation* began to put up large NO PARKING signs along the highway at Maunakea almost as soon as the 2019 protest began (see example in Figure 2.3). The *Hawaii County Police Department* and the *Hawaii State Department of Transportation* then issued a joint statement claiming that the purpose of the signs was to ensure the safety of the traveling public. They added that parking restrictions would be enforced. When protesters claimed that they were being harassed and unfairly targeted in relation to these restrictions, an officer of the *Hawai'i County Police Department* responded by observing that he was unable to corroborate the facts on which the complaint was based because the Department did not keep statistics for the number of citations issued. He added that he had been told that as far as towing cars is concerned, there had been only a few instances (Richardson, August 19, 2019). On August 22, however, *Associated*

Figure 2.3   One of the NO PARKING Signs Put Up by the Hawaiian State Department of Transportation Shortly after the Beginning of the 2019 Maunakea Protest. *Source:* Photo Credit Kaho'okahi Kanuha.

Press reported that police had issued about 100 infringement tickets daily near the site of the protest during the previous week (Finnerty, 2019, August 21).

"Official" presence at the site, and with it, the assumption of ownership and the right to control, is also indicated by the presence of large signs on the clothing of officers of the law (see Figure 2.4). Although it could be argued that signs such as these are necessary in order that people carrying out particular duties can be readily identified, the fact remains that they are often positioned in a way that dominates the immediate landscape, serving to project a sense of permanence, authority and power on the part of the U.S. occupiers and to reinforce the "official" position that the peaceful occupation of their own land by the protesters is somehow transgressive.

While the signs on the clothing of police officers have considerable impact, so too does the traditional clothing worn by some of the protesters, the

Figure 2.4   Sign on Back of a Police Officer at the Maunakea Protest. *Source:* Photo Credit AP Images/Caleb Jones.

draping of bodies in Hawaiian flags and the messages on the clothing of some protesters (see example below):

KANAKA
EXISTENCE—PERSISTENCE
RESISTANCE

In the context of the signs emblazoned on the heavy protective clothing of police, the chosen approach of Hawaiian actor Jason Momoa (see Figure 2.5)[17] is particularly poignant.

In Figure 2.5, Jason Momoa and his young son present their naked torsos as "skinscapes." This is particularly significant when it is borne in mind that the word "skinscape" may refer not only to the physicality of tattooed bodies, but also to their spiritual significance, highlighting what Howes (2018) describes as "the intimate association between the surface of the body and the surface of the earth, or landscape, as found in many non-Western cultures" (p. 229). Referring to an article by Jennifer Biddle (2003), Howes (2018) notes, for example, that "in Aboriginal Australia, the landscape *is* a skinscape: it is composed of the material traces of the bodies of the Ancestral beings who roamed and shaped the countryside during the primordial period referred to

Figure 2.5   Signs on the Naked Bodies of Maunakea Protesters. *Source:* Photo Credit Splash News.

as the Dreaming" (p. 229). In addition, referring to a work by Antonia Mills (2005), he provides (p. 229) an interpreter's translation of testimony presented at a land hearing by a chief of the Wet'suwet'en First Nation[18]:

> If you know the territory well, it is like your own skin. Sometimes you can feel the animals moving on your body as they are on the land, the fish swimming in your bloodstream. . . . If you know the territory well enough, you can feel the animals.

In Hawaiian culture, as in many other Pacific cultures, body art, referred to in Hawai'i as *kākau*, has a variety of purposes. Among them is the signaling of a person's familial and tribal roots and connection with ancestral land.

In Figure 2.5, the word that appears on the naked torso of Jason Momoa's son echoes the last word of the iconic banner displayed in Figure 2.1 above (desecration), the inter-textual referencing adding to the symbolic density of the image. Here, however, the co-text of the word "desecration" is different. On the body of the child, it is presented in a way that highlights the protesters' case in terms of a logical equation (TMT + MAUNAKEA = DESECRATION). What we see here is the power of verbal echo combined with physical choreography. Note the protective positioning of Momoa's hand in relation to the child. Note, too, the positioning of Momoa's head and, in particular, the expression and direction of gaze which suggest suffering combined with awe or reverence directed toward something that is physically and/or metaphysically elevated.

Around Momoa's neck is a *lei* (garland), which appears to be made from the shells of a type of candlenut, the *kukui* (translated as "light") which represents knowledge, wisdom, enlightenment. Knotted into the trailing ends of the lei are leaves of the green *tī* plant, a plant which symbolizes protection in a mystical sense, above all, protection against negative thoughts.[19] The color of the lei and the criss-cross patterning of the weaving, combined with the positioning of the central part around Momoa's throat and the trailing ends, acts as a reminder of one of the most iconographic aspects of slavery— collaring and chaining.

Although it would be disingenuous to suggest that an actor of Momoa's stature was entirely unaware of all of the verbal and visual echoes that are detectable here, he may not have been fully aware of all of them at the time that this photograph was taken. Either way, the result is an image of extraordinary complexity and power.

Another photograph that has been projected around the world is that of a group of seated Hawaiian elders wrapped in blankets against the cold who are blocking the road to the mountain. Behind them is a crowd of protesters, some displaying placards. In the foreground, running in parallel along the middle of the road are double yellow lines (signaling a restriction on passing) which seem to disappear under the bodies of the protesters. In the background is a view of the mountain above which is an expanse of sky. Photographs such as this suggest sophisticated staging that reinforces the impact of verbal signs and highlights very significant aspects of the protest such as the central role played by elders who have fronted the demonstration and have made themselves the main targets of police interventions. For a similar photograph, see Figure 2.6.

Should there be any doubt that a sophisticated awareness of staging and communication are at work among the protesters and their supporters, this is likely to be dispelled by a review of some of the YOU TUBE sites that support and promote their activities. The titles of a few of them are provided below:

Figure 2.6 Maunakea Protest/Protect Group Fronted by Elders. *Source:* Photo credit AP Images/Caleb Jones.

WE ARE MAUNA KEA
Kū Haʻaheo Music Video[20]
Flying back home to Hawaiʻi for MAUNA KEA
Mauna Kea Update: Statement by Puʻuhonua o Puʻuhuluhulu
Mauna kea Protesters welcome New Zealand

Signs at the entrance to the facilities provided by protesters (e.g., MANUNA MEDIC—HEALER HUI) create the impression of a Native Hawaiian settlement, one that is constantly disturbed by the transgressive presence of those who wish to further desecrate the mountain.

Some of the words on other signs that have been in evidence on the mountainside, some appearing many times, either in the same or in slightly different versions, are indicated below:

DESECRATING IS NOT A TRADITION
END U.S. OCCUPATION
NO TREATY NO ANNEXATION NO JURISDICTION NO TMT
PROTECT MAUNAKEA NOW
STOLEN LAND/S
STOP TMT (adapted road sign)
WE WILL NEVER GIVE UP/ TMT WILL NOT BE BUILT
HUMANITY—WE ARE ALL IN THIS TOGETHER
WE ARE MAUNAKEA

Thus far, the signs discussed have been in English or, in the case of the CROWN LANDS sign, in a combination of the English and Hawaiian languages, with the message in the Hawaiian language in smaller print at the bottom of the sign. Some examples of Hawaiian language only signs and Hawaiian and English signs that appeared on the mountainside are reproduced below. Note that although there are some minor errors in Hawaiian in a few of the signs discussed below, attention is not drawn specifically to them since so many Native Hawaiians have had to make so much effort to learn the language to which they should have been entitled.[21]

In Figure 2.7, the two words *Pu'uhuluhulu* and *Pu'uhonua* appear. *Pu'uhuluhulu* is the name of a hill, a large cinder cone, near the place where the protesters are gathered. *Pu'uhonua* is a sanctuary or place of refuge. In Hawaiian tradition, each island had *pu'uhonua*, that is, consecrated places of sanctuary for people escaping from the law or from some form of persecution or threat. Nobody who took sanctuary in a *pu'uhonua* could be touched by any form of authority. Following certain rituals and the elapse of some time, those who took refuge in *pu'uhonua* were set free, able to live their lives without fear of censure.[22] Since it is likely that only those steeped in Hawaiian language and culture are able to appreciate the significance of this sign unless it is explained to them, it appears to be directed almost exclusively toward Native Hawaiian protesters, advising them that they will, ultimately,

Figure 2.7 Sign on Maunakea in the Hawaiian Language. *Source:* Photo credit AP Images/Caleb Jones.

be protected from the power of the forces of oppression. However, for any government or law enforcement officials who *are* able understand, this sign acts as a warning that they should stay away from this place of refuge, a place where Hawaiian culture and identity should remain undisturbed.

In another photograph taken on site (not included here) protesters are executing a Hawaiian version of the New Zealand/Aotearoa Māori *haka*, a war dance traditionally performed in preparation for battle and intended to reinforce determination and bravery on the part of the performers and to instill fear in opponents. The word at the center of a sign held up by one of the protesters (KU'E) can be roughly translated as *Resist*, the words at the top (Eō Lahui Hawai'i) as *Answer the call Hawaiian people*. This is clearly a call to action directed largely at Native Hawaiians. There is also, however, a further message, one that is communicated by implicature: those responsible for the desecration of the mountain and the losses that Native Hawaiians have suffered should not rest easy in their assumption of victory. Resistance may be non-violent but this does not mean that it lacks power, especially in an age where warfare is so often ideological rather than physical.

In Figure 2.8 below, there are signs in Hawaiian (*ALOHA 'ĀINA*) and in English and Hawaiian (PROTECTORS NOT PROTESTERS—*KŪ KIA'I MAUNA;* Protect Mauna kia! Please kohua!!!). The words in the Hawaiian language (in addition to the name of the mountain) that can be seen on the signs can be translated roughly as follows[23]:

ALOHA 'ĀINA = LOVE OF THE LAND
KŪ KIA'I MAUNA = STANDING GUARD/WATCH OVER THE
   MOUNTAIN
Kōkua = help/assist

Some other signs in the Hawaiian language or in English and Hawaiian that appeared from time to time on the mountainside are included below with approximate translations into English:

KIA'I MAUNA—WATCH OVER THE MOUNTAIN
HALEAKALA—Name of the highest mountain on Maui, where there is also
   an observatory that has been the focus of protest in the past.
Ua Lawa Mākou i ka Pōhaku[24]—All we need is the rocks of the land.
BUILD *AHU* NOT TELESCOPES—Build stone temple altars not telescopes.

Three further signs, photographed by Keola Asuncion, a Tahitian language student at the University of Hawai'i at Mānoa, who worked in the kitchen at Maunakea for the guardians, are included here because each of them communicates something that seems to be of particular significance. In the forefront

Figure 2.8   A Group of Protesters on Maunakea with Some Signs in English, One in Hawaiian and Two Signs That Combine English and Hawaiian. *Source:* Photo Credit Jonathan Saupe. Copyright © Hawaii News Now.

of the first of these (see *Figure 2.9* below) are brushes to be used for cleaning shoes before going tramping so as to reduce or eliminate contamination. At the top is an image of the two crossed sticks (*pūlo'ulo'u*) that warn commoners not to enter sacred sites. In large capital letters under the cross pieces is the *'ōlelo no'eau E NIHI KA HELE* (TREAD CAREFULLY), a line from an old-style hula performed from the early 1800s.[25] Apart from the advice/warning in English that hikers should "tread lightly" (followed by an expression of anticipatory thanks in Hawaiian), there is also a reminder in English that one of the things at stake is native habitat. This sign functions as a polite request combined with a warning and a reminder of what is at stake.

In Figure 2.10 below is a placard asserting, in English and in very simple terms, the existential connection between the Native Hawaiian protesters and the mountain (WE ARE Maunakea), and, by association, between Native Hawaiian people generally and their land. Behind these words are a number of messages that seem to be statements or slogans providing encouragement or support. In addition to messages in Hawaiian (e.g., *mālama 'āina* (caring for the land); *aloha 'āina* (love for the land/patriotism)), there is the name of a Māori tribe (*Ngātiwai*), a reminder of the fact that the protest has extended

Figure 2.9   A Sign Provided by Protesters for those Setting Foot on Maunakea. *Source:* Photo Credit and Permission Keola Asuncion.

beyond Hawai'i.[26] One of the interesting aspects of this placard is its graffiti-like character, the levels of superimposition acting as a reminder of the participation, over time, of many different people and peoples, with the statement in the forefront linking them all together in a shared sense of belonging.

Figure 2.11 below shows a placard that includes a portrait of King Kamehameha III who drafted the Hawaiian Kingdom's first constitution in 1840 and sent the first two ambassadors to the UK and France in order to secure official recognition of the Kingdom. The background text is made up of the names of the first group of arrest victims in the Maunakea protest. Above them are the words *UA MAU KE EA O KA 'ĀINA I KA* PONO (SOVEREIGNTY/LIFE ENDURES WHEN ALL IS AS IT SHOULD BE). This is the national slogan of the Hawaiian Kingdom as adopted by Kamehameha III. What we have here is an assertion of the sovereignty of the Hawaiian kingdom, reinforced by the names of some of those who have been prepared to suffer the indignity of arrest on their own land in defense of that sovereignty. The juxtaposition of these names and the portrait of King Kamehameha III also stands as a tribute to those who are named.

Attention has been paid from time to time in the discussion above to some of the speech acts that are evidenced in the contextualized signage. An

Figure 2.10 A Placard Asserting the Intimate Spiritual and Organic Connection between Native Hawaiians and Their Land. *Source:* Photo Credit and Permission Keola Asuncion.

overview of that signage in relation to speech acts highlights some significant aspects of the protest. Thus, for example, in spite of the fact that both *ōlelo Hawai'i* and English are official languages of the 'State of Hawai'i, all of the "official" signs relating to "State authorities" are in English, thus reinforcing the reality of unequal linguistic status. Furthermore, all of these signs take the form of informatives (e.g., *Mauna Kea Science Reserve; POLICE*) or directives, in particular, prohibitives (e.g., NO PARKING), reinforcing the assumption of rightful control.

In the case of signs for which the protesters are responsible, there is considerably more variety in relation to speech acts. With the exception of a few that include other indigenous languages, these signs were found to be in *ōlelo Hawai'i*, English or a mixture of the two. Certainly, there were examples of informatives (e.g., WE ARE HERE TO PROTECT MAUNAKEA), including identifiers that labeled/ named facilities provided *by* protesters *for* protesters. There were also assertions/reminders of the true status of things (e.g., CROWN LANDS). Included in this category (informatives) were those signs which, in the context of Hawaiian culture with its stress on the unity/ connectedness of the human and the non-human, have existential status (e.g., WE ARE MAUNAKEA). Some of the signs combined information

Figure 2.11 A Placard Bearing the Image of King Kamehameha III. *Source:* Photo Credit and Permission Keola Asuncion.

and prohibition (e.g., ROAD CLOSED DUE TO DESECRTATION; STOP TMT). However, an interesting aspect of these signs is that so many were found to be culturally referenced and/or culturally contextualized (by, e.g., the inclusion of cross pieces (*pūlo'ulo'u*)). While some of the words that appear to function as instructions/directions/invitations are clearly aimed at protesters, potential protesters, and sympathizers (e.g., PROTECT MAUNAKEA NOW), others are clearly intended to have a more inclusive appeal (e.g., HUMANITY—WE ARE All IN THIS TOGETHER).

Signs in the Hawaiian language and those parts of signs written in the Hawaiian language function in a number of different ways: signaling Native Hawaiian ownership of the mountain; implicitly affirming the language rights of all linguistically oppressed peoples; acting as a reminder of the official status of the Hawaiian language even according to the statutes of the U.S. occupiers themselves. They provide, in addition, a locus of motivation for Native Hawaiians who do not speak the language of their ancestors. In addition, they communicate culturally specific information and guidance, motivation and instruction and warning (e.g., *PU'UHULUHULU—PU'UHONUA* (CINDER CONE—PLACE OF SANCTUARY); *E NIHI KA HELE* (TREAD CAREFULLY)).

CONCLUSION

Marten et al. (2012) argue that "issues of power and resistance are at the heart of the [LL] research agenda" (p. 1). This is perhaps particularly so where the focus is on a protest movement, as is the case here. Also particularly evident here is the way in which, as indicated in critical discourse theory, some destabilizing crisis can be seen to highlight the contingent nature of the *status quo*, providing a context in which the existing structures of society may be unmasked, disrupted and reconfigured (Laclau & Mouffe, 1985, pp. 111–113). In this case, the proposed building of the TMT is the destabilizing crisis which has led not simply to a small, peaceful, local protest by Native Hawaiians on the side of Maunakea, but to a major global protest movement of indigenous peoples, reinforced by hundreds of thousands of non-indigenous supporters. This movement has, it could be argued, fully, and finally unmasked the illegal occupation of The Hawaiian Kingdom by the United States. In fact, the impact of the Maunakea protest extends further, unmasking some of the lies and deceit that are at the very core of much political posturing worldwide, particularly in relation to the exploitation of animals, peoples, and lands for military or pecuniary advantage. And yet at the center of all of this is a relatively small number of signs, carefully and creatively conceived, positioned and contextualized so as to create a linguistic landscape that resonates throughout the world, particularly at a time when the excesses of industrialization and globalization represent a major threat not only to the majority of surviving languages, cultures, and animal species but also to the very survival of our own species. Rojo (2014, p. 584) has observed that "contemporary social movements have changed spatial forms of gathering and have claimed urban public spaces as sites of resistance." What we see here is Hawai'i's most sacred mountain becoming, in all its natural grandeur, a major site of resistance. What we also see here is the media and social networking sites such as *Facebook* performing a new role. They have represented in the past, and still represent, a serious threat to the maintenance of indigenous languages and cultures. Nevertheless, they can also create spaces where indigenous protesters can share experiences. In doing so, they are able to play a role in the promotion of indigenous causes and contribute to indigenous revival and sustainability.

It is not possible at this point (January 2020) to predict with any degree of certainty what the final outcome of this protest will be. On December 26, 2019 protesters were ordered to clear the road or face arrest (Dayton, 2019). Having received an assurance that there would be no building work associated with the telescope before the end of February 2020, protesters/protectors agreed to move their major tent (*Kupuna* tent) to the side of the road in order that the road could be reopened. They indicated, however, that they would not abandon their protection of the mountain (Hawai'i News Now, 2019). Whatever the final outcome in relation to the TNT, one thing we know for sure is that from January 1, 2020 (a) all public acts and transactions were to be made available in the Hawaiian language; and (b) all reasonable efforts were to be taken to make government records, papers or documents available in the Hawaiian language. A small achievement, but an achievement nevertheless. The fact that it is now widely known that the United States is an illegal occupier of the Kingdom of Hawai'i is, however, a far greater achievement. In connection with this, the National Lawyers Guild[27] has called on the United States to begin to comply with international humanitarian law in its long and illegal occupation of the Hawaiian islands (National Lawyers Guild, 2019).

NOTES

1. The size of these eight islands is as follows: *Hawai'i* (10,430 km²), *O'ahu* (1,545 km²), *Maui* (1,883 km²), *Kaua'i* (1,456 km²), *Moloka'i* (670 km²), *Lāna'i* (364 km²), *Ni'ihau* (180 km²), and *Kaho'olawe* (116.47 km²)

2. Assurance of recognition of the Kingdom's independence was given by President John Tyler of the United States (December 19, 1842), King Louis-Philippe of France (March 17th, 1843) and Lord Aberdeen, on behalf of Queen Victoria (April 1, 1843). On November 28, 1843, the British and French Governments formally recognized Hawaiian independence in a joint declaration by France and Britain, signed by King Louis-Philippe and Queen Victoria (*The Anglo-Franco Proclamation*).

3. *The Reciprocity Treaty* of 1875 had provided Hawaiian exporters with advantageous terms in relation to trade with the United States. This was rescinded by the *McKinley Tariff*. In response, Queen Lili'uokalani proposed a lottery and opium licensing to bring in additional revenue. These controversial proposals were later used against her.

4. The alphabetic system has changed over time and there are now five vowels (a; e; i; o; u) and eight consonants (h; k; l; m; n; p; w; '). The last of these consonants ('), called the 'okina, has no capital form and so the following letter is capitalized where a capital is required. Long vowels have a macron (or kahakō) above them: ā ; ē ; ī ; ō; ū. There are eleven diphthongs (ai (kai: sea water); ae (mae'ole = never-fading); ao (maoli = true); au (au = I/ I am); ei (lei = garland); eu ('eleu = lively); iu (wēkiu = topmost); oe ('oe = you); oi (poi = type of food, usually made from cooked taro corms); ou (kou = your); ui (hui = together/team/chorus)).

5. Section 103 reads (in part): For purposes of this title—(1) The term "Native American" means an Indian, Native Hawaiian, or Native American Pacific Islander.

6. This was in spite of the fact that at least four and a half thousand students were learning the Hawaiian language or learning through the medium of Hawaiian language at that time.

7. Elizabeth Sinclair purchased Niʻihau in 1864 for $10,000 from The Kingdom of Hawaii. Private ownership was passed on to her descendants, the Robinson family.

8. Niʻihau residents move freely between Niʻihau and Kauaʻi and a few Hawaiian-speaking families who are relatives of Niʻihau residents are to be found in Kauaʻi and other islands.

9. There are believed to be fewer than two thousand native speakers, all above sixty years of age, scattered throughout Oʻahu, Molokaʻi, Hawaiʻi, Lānaʻi, Maui, and Kauaʻi.

10. For a discussion of the blossoming of Hawaiian-controlled education in the Hawaiian language and through the medium of the Hawaiian language, see, for example, Schütz (1994); Walk (2008).

11. Associate Professor of Hawaiian studies at the University of Hawaiʻi

12. Professor of Law (Geneva School of Diplomacy), former Secretary of the UN Human Rights Committee and at that time UN Independent Expert on the promotion of democratic and equitable international order

13. The complaint was submitted by Mme Routh Bolomet.

14. *Mise en abyme* is the name given to a formal technique in art of placing a copy of an image within itself, often many times, in a way that is suggestive of infinite recursion.

15. Thanks to Dr. Richard Keaoopuaokalani NeSmith for this information.

16. Maile Arvin is a native Hawaiian feminist scholar who is Assistant Professor of history and gender studies at the University of Utah.

17. Jason Momoa (Joseph Jason Namakaeha Momoa) is a Hawaiian actor, director, writer, and producer who was born in Honolulu.

18. Located in what is now British Colombia.

19. Thanks to Dr. Richard Keaoopuaokalani NeSmith for information about the composition of the lei and the significance of the inclusion of green *tī* plant.

20. This music video is inspired by events on Maunakea.

21. Some errors were pointed out to me by Dr. Richard Keaoopuaokalani NeSmith

22. Thanks to Dr. Richard Keaoopuaokalani NeSmith for information about the meaning and significance of *Puʻuhuluhulu* and *Puʻuhonua*.

23. Capital letters have been retained where they appeared on the signs included here.

24. These words are from a proverb (*ʻōlelo noʻeau*) that occurs in a song composed for Queen Liliʻuokalani after the rebels and US marines deposed her in 1893. Thanks to Dr. Richard Keaoopuaokalani for this information.

25. Dr. Richard Keaoopuaokalani NeSmith provided the translation and origin of the words in this sign and also noted that the old-style hula is still performed, but with a tune that was modernized in the late 1800s. He also supplied translations of the Hawaiian words included in the other signs discussed.

26. Present among the protesters have been Māori, Tahitians, Tongans, Samoans, Fijians, and Aboriginal Australians.

27. The *National Lawyers Guild* is the oldest and largest progressive bar association in the United States of America.

Chapter 3

Aotearoa/New Zealand: Tirau

A Twenty-First Century Colonial Fantasy Landscape

INTRODUCTION AND BACKGROUND

Location and Population

Aotearoa/New Zealand[1] is located in the south-western Pacific Ocean, 2,000 km east of Australia and approximately 1,000 km south of the New Caledonian archipelago. It is made up of a large number of islands covering 267,701 km^2, the largest of which are the North Island (*Te Ika-a-Māui*), the South Island (*Te Waipounamu*), and Stewart Island (*Rakiura*). New Zealand has a wealth of mountains, rainforests, sandy beaches, fjords, and fertile farm land. It also has many active volcanos, with a high frequency of eruptions. Although it has only two native land mammals (both types of bat) and no snakes, it does have many marine mammals, including dolphins, seals, whales and porpoises, many bird, and insect species (some flightless), approximately 2,500 native plant varieties and almost 6,000 types of fungi as well as native frogs, eels, water snails, and crayfish.

The estimated population of New Zealand is now approximately 5 million people.[2] Of these, approximately 74 percent are of European ethnicity, 15 percent of indigenous Māori ethnicity, 12 percent of Asian ethnicity, and 7 percent of Pacific Islands ethnicity[3] (Statistics New Zealand, n.d.).[4] The capital city, Wellington (*Te Whanganui-a-Tara*), with a population of just over 400,000, is the location of central government, most public service administration and many cultural organizations. The largest city is, however, Auckland (*Tāmaki Makaurau*), a cosmopolitan city with an urban population of just over 1.6 million.

The country has two official languages *de jure* (the Māori language (since 1987) and New Zealand sign language (since 2006)) and one official language *de facto* (English). However, although over 96 percent of New Zealanders claim to be able to hold a conversation about everyday things in the English language, and just under one fifth claim to speak more than one language, only approximately 3 percent of the population as a whole maintain that they are able to hold a conversation about everyday things in the Māori language. This includes just over 21 percent of those of Māori ethnicity (Statistics New Zealand, n.d.).

The country was first settled between 1200 and 1300 CE by migrants from East Polynesia. By 1300, a large change from predominantly forest to bracken, fern and scrub, with an increase in charcoal, indicates the burning of forests to create spaces for living and cultivation and, hence, the establishment of community settlements (Irwin & Walrond, n.d). In common with many other Polynesian communities, traditional Māori communities included skilled navigators, astronomers, tool makers, hunters, fishers, food gatherers, and cultivators as well as oral historians. Among traditional Māori cultural art forms were oratory, song and dance (including war dances such as the *haka*), wood carving, flax weaving, and tattooing. As Biggs (1968, p. 77) observes, "[a] great body of myth, legend and historical tradition was passed down the generations in prose narrative, sung poetry and genealogical recital."

The Dutch navigator Abel Tasman may have been the first European explorer to sight New Zealand and chart part of the coastline (December 1642). However, Captain James Cook, a British explorer and navigator, was almost certainly the first European to circumnavigate the land (October 1769). By the late 1700s, New Zealand waters were being visited by adventurers as well as by whalers and sealers from Britain, France, and the United States and ships' crews were trading European goods for food, water, wood, and flax. By the early 1800s, missionaries and European settlers had begun to make inroads into the country, establishing mission stations, developing a written script for the Māori language and laying claim to parcels of land. In 1839, the New Zealand Company, chartered in London and aiming to systematically colonize New Zealand, announced plans to buy large tracts of land to sell to the increasing number of settlers. This, combined with the lawlessness of some of the settlers and visiting seamen and the increased interest in the land by the French, led to a growing sense of the need for regulation and, hence, to Britain's decision to annex the country. Captain William Hobson, a Royal Navy officer, was sent to New Zealand with instructions to persuade Māori to cede their sovereignty to the British Crown. Treaty notes were put together by Hobson and his secretary James Freeman, tidied up by James Busby, British Resident in New Zealand, and, over one evening, translated into the Māori language (te reo Māori) by missionary Henry Williams and his son Edward. On February 6, 1840, forty Māori chiefs signed the Treaty at a meeting at Waitangi in the North Island and copies were then taken around the county for further signing. In fact, however, many Māori chiefs did not sign or were not even invited to do so.

Almost all aspects of the Treaty of Waitangi have been the subject of ongoing dispute and disagreement (Orange, 1987). There are, for example, fundamental differences between the ways in which the English language version and the Māori language version have been interpreted, with only the English language version, which was not the one Māori were invited to sign, unambiguously involving the ceding of sovereignty to Britain. There have also been disputes about the ways in which the signatures of Māori chiefs were obtained. What cannot, however, be disputed is the fact that even the English version of the Treaty guarantees to Māori "full exclusive and undisturbed possession of their Lands and Estates Forests Fisheries and other properties which they may collectively or individually possess so long as it is their wish and desire to retain the same in their possession" (*Te Tiriti o Waitangi/Treaty of Waitangi,* 1840). Even so, from 1840 onward, the situation of Māori began to deteriorate significantly.

New Zealand is now an independent nation and has been, to all intents and purposes, since 1852 when, only twelve years after the signing of the *Treaty of Waitangi,* the British government passed the *New Zealand Constitution Act*[5] (later repealed by the *Constitution Act* of *1986*) according to which the colony's settlers (not the indigenous people) were granted the right to self-governance. The first election was held in 1853 and from 1867, all Māori men were accorded the right to vote. These facts cannot, however, be taken at face value. If Britain did not have any real right to assume control over the country, neither did it have the right to cede that control in favor of the settlers.

The devastating impact of colonization on the Māori population continued. The settlers, eventually massively superior in terms of numbers, were now effectively in control. In 1919, New Zealand were invited to join the League of Nations.[6] In 1926, any technical issues remaining in relation to the independence of Britain's former colonies was resolved by the passing of the *Balfour Declaration,* according to which Britain's "dominions" were accorded equal legal status with Britain itself. This was followed in 1931 by the passing of *The Statute of Westminster* which provided for the removal of any possible basis for Britain's intervention in the government of former colonies and established the *Commonwealth of Nations.* It was not, however, until 1947 that New Zealand adopted the statute (the *Statute of Westminster Adoption Act 1947*). Following that, in 1949, it became a member of the *Commonwealth of Nations,* a group aiming to promote peace and prosperity which is now made up of Britain and fifty-two countries, most former British colonies, of which sixteen (including New Zealand) retain the British monarch as their Head of State, something which is of symbolic significance only.

None of this, however, alters the fact that New Zealand is a country whose indigenous people, as a result of colonization, have been denied the right to determine their own destiny.

The Indigenous People: Culture, Language, Poverty, and Alienation

Classical Māori culture (*Māoritanga*), that is, the culture that obtained before widespread European contact, had much in common with that of Eastern Polynesian societies generally. There were, however, differences, not only between Māori and other Eastern Polynesian societies but also among different Māori tribal groups (Belich, 1996). Nevertheless, some generalizations are possible. For Māori, all things, including human beings and natural phenomena, were linked through genealogy and all possessed a life force (*mauri*) which could be expressed in the form of powerful symbolic presences. Thus, for example, Tangaroa was the life force and ancestor of fish and the oceans, Rongo was the life force and ancestor of plants and agriculture. Some things were considered to be imbued with spiritual power (*mana*) and were, therefore, subject to certain rules and prohibitions (*tapu*), the violation of which could have serious consequences, including death. Life was organized along tribal lines, with tribes (*iwi*), headed by chiefs (*rangatira*), being made up of several related clans (*hapū*), which were, in turn, made up of several related extended family groups (*whanau*) led by elders (*kaumātua*). Land was passed down through generations by continuous occupation.

In 1840, at the time of the signing of the *Treaty of Waitangi*, the number of British settlers was approximately 2,000. Within just over three decades, it had risen to around 46,000 (Christiansen, 2001, pp. 15–16). When Europeans first arrived in New Zealand, there were approximately 100,000 Māori (Belich, 1986, p. 300) living in tribal groups which had an intricate social structure and effective ways of passing knowledge and information from generation to generation (Nock, 2010, p. 185). Within five or six decades of the signing of the Treaty, that number had fallen to around 42,000 due to introduced diseases, land loss and social and cultural disruption. Within ten decades of the signing, Māori had lost approximately 99 percent of their land in the South Island and 91 percent in the North Island (Ministry for Culture and Heritage (NZ), 2015).

In 1840, almost all communication involving Māori took place through the medium of the Māori language (Spolsky, 2003, pp. 555–556). Within ten years, Māori were proportionately more literate than European settlers (Ka'ai-Mahuta, 2011, p. 200). By the 1970s, however, very few Māori children (approximately 5 percent) could speak the Māori language (Belich,

1986, pp. 299–300; Salmon, 1991, pp. 95–97; Waitangi Tribunal, 1986, p. 11). By that time, Māori were seriously under-represented in terms of economic and educational success and over-represented in terms of statistics relating to poverty, ill health, and crime (Nock, 2010, p. 187).

So far as the Māori language is concerned, a range of social and political circumstances led to its decline. Just seven years after the signing of the *Treaty of Waitangi*, an act was passed which specified that only educational instruction conducted through the medium of English would be given financial support by government (*Education Ordinance Act* 1847). This was followed by the *Native Schools Act 1858* and *1867* which placed all Māori schools under government control. The use of the Māori language on school grounds was prohibited and subject to punishment. Observing that it was in the interests of their children to learn English, Māori parents began to encourage the use of English at home. The impact of all of this was intensified by a drift from rural to urban living that resulted from loss of land and loss of employment opportunities in the countryside. This, together with "pepper-potting," the habit of placing Māori families in predominantly non-Māori areas to facilitate assimilation, meant not only the loss of social support networks but also of Māori language networks. Thus: "On radio, on television, in the newspapers, on road signs, everywhere they turned, Māori were subjected to the impact of the dominant language" (Nock, 2014, pp. 16–17).

From the 1970s onwards, Māori resistance, in spite of considerable setbacks, began to have an effect both culturally and linguistically. In 1972, a group of young Māori academics initiated a petition that called for the inclusion of Māori language in the school curriculum. That petition attracted over 300,000 signatures (Brooking, 1988, p. 191). In 1976, the first bilingual school was opened and soon after, thanks to a combination of militancy and peaceful persuasion on the part of Māori, Māori language pre-schools and Māori immersion schools were flourishing, the Māori language was being made available in some mainstream primary and secondary schools, Māori studies, including Māori language tuition, was being made available in polytechnics and universities, and Māori tertiary institutions were an established part of the educational scene (Walker, 2004, pp. 210–212).

In 1975, a permanent commission of enquiry, *The Waitangi Tribunal*, was set up to investigate Māori claims relating to perceived breaches of the terms of the *Treaty of Waitangi* and to make recommendations to government in connection with compensation in the case of claims judged to be valid. In 1984, the Tribunal ruled that the Māori language should be considered a "possession" under the terms of the Treaty and should, therefore, be given official recognition and protection (Waitangi Tribunal, 1986, p. 6). As a result, an act was passed giving official status to the Māori language and establishing a *Māori Language Commission* (*Te Taura Whiri i te Reo Māori*) to oversee its protection (*Māori Language Act* 1987). Even so, in and of itself, that Act has had little impact in terms of extending the number of domains in which the language is spoken on a day-to-day basis. In fact, the act guarantees little more than the right to speak the Māori language in certain legal settings using registered translators. Thus, in spite of all the progress that Māori have made, the state of the Māori language remains fragile, with an ongoing lack of effective support for tribal dialects and for inter-generational transmission (Waitangi Tribunal, 2001, p. 441 & 442).

REALITY VERSUS MYTHOLOGY

In contemporary New Zealand, approximately 86 percent of people live in urban areas and approximately one fifth were born overseas (Statistics New Zealand, n.d.). In spite of this, and in spite of the country's proud Māori heritage, New Zealand identity is still often thought of almost wholly in terms of a colonial past in which "the work of clearing the bush and 'breaking in' the land was seen as central to the process of building a nation" (Sinclair, 1986, p. 8). Associated with this, corrugated iron and number eight fencing wire, used widely in rural areas as make-do building roofing and fencing materials, have become national icons. Used initially as a general all-purpose resource in rural areas, corrugated iron tended initially to appear in urban areas only on parts of buildings that were generally hidden. At the beginning of the twentieth century, however, it began to be widely used for roofing in both rural and urban settings and has more recently come to be associated with a nostalgic and functionalist architectural style (Kiwi Crazy, 2010).

THE SITE AND THE REASONS FOR ITS SELECTION

Writing almost a decade ago, Macalister (2010) observed that "for most non-Māori New Zealanders knowledge of the Māori language primarily entails familiarity with a range of borrowings from Māori into English" (p. 58). In a study of signs in a street in the South Island of New Zealand, located in an area which attracts visitors and tourists, Macalister found that there were no signs in the Māori language and no bilingual signs" (p. 69). However, as 86 percent of Māori live in the North Island (Statistics New Zealand, n. d.), I was interested to find out whether the situation was similar there. I, therefore, selected for investigation of its signage a North Island township called Tirau which has a slightly larger proportion of Māori residents than has the country as a whole—approximately 27.7 percent as compared 16.5

percent (Statistics New Zealand, n.d.)—and which also has a range of shops and other commercial ventures that attract both New Zealand and overseas visitors and tourists.

Tirau is a small rural township in the North Island of New Zealand. It was established as a township in the 1860s when blocks of land in the area were developed by European settlers for cattle grazing. Early plans for the area indicated that the intention was to create something similar to an English cathedral city (Tirau info., n.d.). In the 1880s, a post and telegraph office, named *Okoroire*, and a hotel, named *The Oxford Royal*, were opened. In 1890, the name of the post and telegraph office was changed to *Oxford* (after the English town of that name) and the name was extended to the township. Later, however, after another New Zealand township began to be referred to by the same name, the name was changed once again, this time to *Oxford North*. In 1896, the current name, *Tirau*, was adopted. This name is widely believed to have been borrowed from the Māori name for a prominent hill in the area where many cabbage trees (*Ti* = cabbage tree; *rau* = many) provided an overnight roosting site for native pigeons (*kereu*) and, hence, a rich source of food for the local Māori people of the Ngati Raukawa tribe whose people had established villages in the area and were responsible for extensive terracing of the surrounding hills. In giving the township this name, the residents acknowledged its Māori heritage and, no doubt, also acknowledged the fact that that the settlers' initial lofty ambition to create a large city similar to Oxford in England were extremely unlikely to be realized.

Tirau gradually became a thriving rural service center. At the end of the 1980s, however, its residents were obliged to come to terms with a destabilizing crisis. The township experienced a rapid and severe decline resulting from a combination of public sector restructuring and a widespread economic downturn which followed Britain's entry into the European Economic Community and its staged withdrawal from special import/export agreements with New Zealand. This was exacerbated by a range of government policies which removed agricultural subsidies, further exposing the agricultural sector and leading to a spike in suicides as farmers were forced from their land (Wallace, 2014).[7] Tirau lost its place as a local county administrative center and its role as a rural service center and most of its shops and services were closed. This could have been the end of the line for the township. But Tirau survived. One factor that played a very important role in that survival was the gradual emergence of New Zealand as a tourist destination.

In the 1980s, tourism was beginning to have an impact on New Zealand[8] and Tirau was well placed geographically to benefit from this. Situated 50 km southeast of Hamilton[9] (New Zealand's fourth largest city), it is located at a major junction in the New Zealand State Highway network where traffic from Auckland[10] (New Zealand's largest city) or Hamilton can head for the major tourist attractions available in Taupo,[11] Rotorua,[12] and the Coromandel Peninsula[13]. Even so, Tirau seemed to have little hope of competing for tourist dollars. It was, after all, a small rural township bifurcated by a main road as indicated in the two photographs below, one taken from the beginning of the main through road, the other from a position approximately 5 m back from the main through road (See Figure 3.1).

In spite of its essentially rural character, the township began, in the 1990s, to re-emerge as a tourist destination, beginning when a local entrepreneur turned an empty store into a successful antique business and an old council building into a conference and events center. In 1994, by the side of the main road through Tirau, a wool and textile craft shop was constructed out of corrugated iron in the shape of an enormous sheep.[14] Four years later, a toilet block and information center, also made out of corrugated iron, but this time in the shape of a large dog, was also constructed (see Figure 3.2).

What we see here is the beginning of Tirau's commercial development, a development that clearly had an impact on its landscape in ways that

Figure 3.1   Photographs Taken From and Near Tirau's Main through Road. *Source:* Photo Credit Diane Johnson.

Figure 3.2   "Big Dog" Toilet Block and Information Centre and "Big Sheep" Wool Gallery, Tirau, New Zealand. *Source:* Photo Credit Diane Johnson.

reflect both Hughes' (1992) observation that tourism entrepreneurs can crate mythical places, disregarding their real historical dynamics and the more general observation by Figueiredo and Raschi (2011, p. 2/82) that "new symbolic values and social meanings are [increasingly] being attributed to rural areas."

Writing in the early 2000s, Panelli et al. (2003) noted that Tirau had changed "from a conventional, small, service center to become a . . . consumption-focused 'destination'" (p. 386).[15] Since that time, a large corrugated iron ram has joined the sheep and, transforming the landscape, large, whimsical corrugated iron signs have appeared in association with almost all of the commercial enterprises located on the main through road and adjacent areas. Tirau now has a range of cafés and restaurants, and a variety of shops specializing in antiques, crafts and locally and nationally produced gifts, clothing, and homeware. There is also, although approximately 3.5 km from the center of the township, a large privately run museum. The residents of Tirau had found a route to survival in the face of enormous odds.

So far as tourism in Aoteraoa/New Zealand as a whole is concerned, Māori now play a central role, owning and operating many tourist facilities, providing cultural artifacts, such as authentic bone and wood carvings for the tourist market and, above all, creating a unique sense of place. Since Tirau was originally a Māori settlement, with Māori having been the first to farm the land, one would expect them to be writ large in this new tourist-focused landscape.

THE LINGUISTIC LANDSCAPE OF TIRAU'S COMMERCIAL AREA

Introduction

I visited Tirau many times during a two-month period in 2016[16] and again in 2018. In 2016, I paid particular attention to signage on, or adjacent to, the main through road and streets adjoining it, where almost all of the township's commercial outlets are located. I noted first that all of the signs relating to the flow of traffic were in English only (as is the case in every part of New Zealand I have visited). I then identified and photographed all signs, pictorial and/or linguistic, associated with the naming of streets and the naming/branding of commercial and community establishments as well as any other signs that appeared outside these properties or in their street-facing windows. When I visited the township again in 2018, I was interested to see whether there had been any major changes in the landscape of the commercial area of the township.

In terms of the immediate context in which these signs appeared, one of the first things of which I became aware was a *tino rangatiratanga* flag (representing Māori sovereignty) which could be seen flying from a private dwelling located on a side road leading off of the main through road.

Street Names

The main road that runs directly through Tirau (State Highway 1) is called *Main Street.* Most of the other streets in Tirau are named after local landscape features (*Hillcrest Street*; *Prospect Avenue*) or buildings or constructions of various types (e.g., *Church Street*; *Station Street*; *Bridge Street*), a few of the referenced features being no longer in evidence. One street, *Rose Street*, is named after a prominent local colonial family. Two have names associated with the township in the past. One of these, *Oxford Street*, recalls the cathedral city in which England's oldest university is located and, with it, the aspirations of some of the early European settlers; the other, *Okoroire Street*, makes reference to the township's Māori heritage. The name of that street, meaning "place of the *koreoire*" in the Māori language, acts as a reminder, for those familiar with local history, of the fact that a type of native duck (*koroire*), now extinct, was once prevalent in the area. With the exception of the current name of the township itself, this was the only evidence of the Māori language that was detected in the street names in the area surveyed.

The Naming of Commercial Establishments

When the main part of this study was conducted in 2016, there were two community structures (the Tirau war memorial hall and the Tirau community church) and fifty-eight commercial premises in the area surveyed. Among the commercial establishments displaying their names on signs above their window displays were:

- Two branches of international commercial operations: *Subway* (fast food chain); *BP* (petrol station chain);
- One New Zealand-based company that is now operating internationally: *Bendon* (lingerie); and
- Three New Zealand-based companies operating in a range of locations in the country: *The Carpenter's Daughter* (plus sized women's clothing); *Ebony* (women's clothing); *The Christmas Heirloom Company.*

The remainder of the commercial establishments appeared to be specific to Tirau (although some also had an online presence). Some of them had English names which could appear almost anywhere in New Zealand (e.g.,

The Honey Shop Café). Some appeared to be named after their owners (e.g., *Georgia Brown Gifts*; *Ronnies Café*). The remainder can be grouped under three headings:

- those that included the current name of the township;
- those that made reference, direct or indirect, to somewhere beyond the current township and set up some type of humorous contrast between the place to which reference is made and the township itself; and
- those that involved humor or whimsy that was not based on contrast.

The establishments in the first group above (see example in Figure 3.3) appeared to cater largely to local people and to lack the type of elaborate frontage and signage that was associated with many of the more tourist-focused commercial establishments.

The establishments in the second group above all made reference, directly or indirectly, to distant places, places associated with settings and cultures that would generally be regarded as exotic and sophisticated. The contrast between these places and Tirau itself is one aspect of a type of self-mocking humor that pervades the recreated landscape. Among the names in the second group are *The Oxford Café, The Merchant of Tirau*, and *Notting Hill Interiors*.

Figure 3.3 Tirau Home Kills Sign. *Source:* Photo Credit Diane Johnson.

The Oxford Café, situated on the main through road, takes its name from the time when Tirau was named after the city in which England's oldest university is located, a city in which students are still sometimes required to wear academic robes and one in which a characteristic mode of student transport is the bicycle. Hence a robed figure on a bicycle on the café sign and as an embossed window sign (see Figure 3.4). The name and the accompanying image highlight the contrast between the two locations and, for those who are aware of the township's history, serves as an ironic reminder of the early grand plans for the township.

Another establishment name that comes into the second category is *The Merchant of Tirau*. This name appeared in Blackadder font, sometimes referred to as "Gothic" or "Old English." The name, combined with the nature of the merchandise (high end, including gourmet groceries) and the way in which that merchandise was presented (e.g., wine bottles displayed in wooden cases packed with straw), appeared to reinforce what is likely, for some, to be an evocation of Shakespeare's *Merchant of Venice* and, with it, the historic city of Venice, a World Heritage Site. The implicit contrast between Tirau and Venice is highlighted in a further contrast, that is, the contrast between the elegant presentation of the shop itself and a hand printed sign in the window advising customers to remove their muddy shoes (see

Figure 3.4   The Oxford Café, Tirau. *Source:* Photo Credit Diane Johnson.

Figure 3.5 Sign in the Window of The Merchant of Tirau. *Source:* Photo Credit Diane Johnson.

Figure 3.5), a sign that indicates the rural/ farming nature of the shop's setting and something of the rural reality behind the sophisticated commercial setting.

Opened in 2004 in Tirau, *Notting Hill Interiors,* like *The Merchant of Tirau,* appeared to be aiming for a high-end clientele. It is described in its online site as being named after the owner's "favourite place in London" and as providing an "iconic destination store" offering "classic sophisticated European styling and timeless ranges of furniture, stunning collections of homewares, décor items, gorgeous jewellery and accessories" (Notting Hill Interiors, n.d.). Located in one of the most densely populated urban boroughs in the UK, and with some of the UKs most elegant and expensive properties, Notting Hill could not present a starker contrast with the small, rural township of Tirau.

The third group of signs referred to above includes *The Alley Cats Café, The Handle Bar, Antiques @ Tirau,* and *The Bugger Café.*

The Alley Cats Café, with a corrugated iron sign depicting a skinny black cat, is located in a narrow alleyway; *The Handle Bar,* with the name printed on a corrugated iron sign underneath a picture of a long, upward curving moustache, relies for its impact on the contrast between a handle of beer[17] and a type of moustache that was particularly associated with the "Wild West" of the United States in the latter part of the nineteenth century[18]; the name *Antiques @ Tirau* highlights the contrast between the antiquity of what is being sold and the modern Internet-based usage of the central symbol. *The Bugger Café* (see Figure 3.6) has a name with a range of associations. For New Zealanders, the word "bugger" is often now particularly associated with one of the country's most iconic television advertisements, a Toyota commercial from the late 1990s, widely known as the "bugger ad," which drew upon a particular type of understated Kiwi humor to refer to a number of farming mishaps. Appearing in the advertisement (Toyota Hilux advertisement, 1999) is a red tractor, similar to the one which is located, as if abandoned on a pile of rubble, below the shop sign.

Images Accompanying the Names of Shop Signs

The images represented on the corrugated iron signs associated with shops in Tirau included a mouse with a bunch of grapes and a piece of cheese (*The Merchant of Tirau*), poppy flowers (*Poppys Café*), a gowned figure on a bicycle (*The Oxford Café*), a flock of birds (*The Enchanted Café*), a heart (*Sami gift store*), a goose (*The Loose Goose Café*), an ice cream cone and a liquorice allsorts man (*La More Sweets*), a teapot (*Heidis on the hill Café*), a giraffe, a monkey, an elephant, and a tiger (*On Safari*), a cartoon man wearing an apron (*The Merchant of Tirau*), a cat (*The Alley Cats Café*), a cow

Figure 3.6   Bugger Café, Tirau. *Source:* Photo Credit Diane Johnson.

(*Tirau Foodmarket*), a sunflower wearing sunglasses (*Outdoor Obsession*), a car with two feet protruding from the chassis (*Tirau Motors Ltd.*), and two stylized pukeko birds, one wearing a necklace (*Silver & some—Figure 3.7*). Of these, only the gowned figure on a bicycle, the cow and the pukeko birds (one of the most widely recognized of New Zealand's native birds), could be seen as having any particular relevance so far as the township of Tirau and/ or the country as a whole are concerned.

Māori Words and Images Displayed on Signs in the Area Surveyed

On a board outside the information center, there was a greeting in the Māori language: *Haere mai* with an English translation underneath (see Figure 3.8).

Apart from the very few evidences of the Māori language in the signage surveyed, there were only two indications of pre-European occupation of the area. The first, an indirect one, was in the name of one of the cafés—*The Cabbage Tree Café*—which involves translation from the Māori language into English of part of the current name of the township (*Ti* = cabbage tree). In fact, the name of one of the commercial outlets—*Tirau Shell & Jade*— included the word "jade" (rarely used in New Zealand) rather than its New Zealand English equivalent (*greenstone*) or its Māori name (*pounamu*).[19] Even so, the second indication of pre-European occupation was to be found

Figure 3.7 A Corrugated Iron Sign above Silver & Some, Tirau. *Source:* Photo Credit Diane Johnson.

Figure 3.8   Sign Outside the Information Centre in Tirau. *Source:* Photo Credit Diane Johnson.

Figure 3.9   Some Further Examples of Signs in the Commercial Area of Tirau. *Source:* Photo Credit Diane Johnson.

in images on a sign outside that shop which were of carved objects that are readily associated with Māori culture—a fish hook (symbolizing health and prosperity), intertwined ferns (symbolizing the bond between people), and an unfurling silver fern (symbolizing hope and new beginnings).

Some Further Observations on Signage

The role that humor and whimsy play in Tirau's commercial presentation is evidenced not only in the naming and image branding of some of its commercial operations but also in a range of other signs associated with these operations (see examples in Figure 3.9). Nor is humor and whimsy confined to the commercial domain. However, none of this appears to have provided the township with a secure commercial future. Of the fifty-eight commercial establishments in the area surveyed, twelve (approximately 20 percent), including the *Big Sheep Wool Gallery*, were empty and/or advertised as being for sale or lease at the time this study was conducted.

Semi-Structured Interviews

A number of standardized open-ended (semi-structured) interviews were conducted with visitors to Tirau. Although these interviews could take a number of directions depending on the interviewees, certain questions were always included at some point. These questions related to interviewees' perceptions of the nature and function of the signage in the main street and adjacent areas. Twelve interviews were conducted, involving six New Zealanders (two of whom were of Māori descent) and six overseas visitors (two from Taiwan, one from Scotland, one from England, one from India, and one from Korea). These were people who were in Tirau on Saturdays during the two-month period when I conducted the main part of the study reported here.

Table 3.1 below provides an overview of interview questions relating to signage and responses to these questions.

As indicated in the table above, although all of the interviewees appeared to like the corrugated iron signs in and around Tirau and most believed that their primary function was a commercial one, they also appeared, in general, to believe that there was no particular reason why certain animals and birds were represented on the signs. Even so, a majority (all of the New Zealand interviewees and one Asian visitor), appeared to be aware of the iconic role that corrugated iron plays in New Zealand identity construction (see the following interview extracts from interviewees as indicated in the Table above):

> *Corrugated iron is a NZ thing. Think about Jeff Thomson's corrugated cows. And there's that massive corrugated iron gumboot at Taihape and corrugated iron kiwi birds around Otorohanga.*
>
> *It's like number eight fencing wire. It's a New Zealand thing.*
>
> *It's cheap and cheerful. We New Zealanders like to think that we make the best of what we have—so, yes, I think that the corrugated iron says "This is New Zealand."*

A majority of the interviewees did not believe that the shop names and signs communicated anything about Tirau's history. However, one of them, a Māori New Zealander, responded as follows:

Table 3.1 Overview of Questions and Responses Relating to Tirau's Signage. Author created

What do you think about the corrugated iron signs and buildings around Tirau?	*Like (x10)* *Like but a bit over the top (x1)* *Like but wouldn't like to live with them (x1)*
Do you think the corrugated iron signs are intended to have a function?	*Yes—commercial—attract visitors (x9)* *Don't know (x2)* *Just funny (x1)*
Do you think there is a reason why some of the signs depict particular birds or animals?	*People like animals (x9)* *Don't know (x2)* *Can't be a reminder of rural NZ because there are elephants and giraffes (x1)* *Added comments:* *I think it's probably just a bit random;* *The sheep and the dog are very rural NZ;* *Could it be animals you get in the area?*
Do you think the fact that these signs are made out of corrugated iron has any particular significance?	*Don't know (x3)* *A New Zealand thing (x9)* *Added comments:* *References to other corrugated iron arts and crafts, to number eight fencing wire, and to low cost (see below).*
Do you think that the shop names and signs in the main street of Tirau tell you anything about the history of the area?	*Don't know (x4)* *No (x3)* *Some connection with Oxford and/or London? (x3)* *Some signs reflect the fact that it used to be called Oxford (x1)* *One response referring to lack of a Māori presence (see below).*
Is there anything else about the signs in and around Tirau that you think and would like to share?	*Two comments added (see below)*

There's Tirau home kills and a Tirau food market and there's a cabbage tree café. Otherwise, the whole of the main area of town seems to say nothing about the Māori who lived here and still do.

Asked to add anything they wished about signs in Tirau, two of the interviewees added comments (see below). The first comment was provided by an Asian visitor, the second by the second Māori New Zealander:

I just wonder what the local people—apart from the shopkeepers—think of them.
Well Tirau is a Māori name but there's not much that's Māori about the place that I can see.

A Later (2018) Addition to Tirau's Signage

My primary exploration of the linguistic landscape of Tirau's main commercial area was conducted in 2016. When I returned in 2018, in addition to some changes to the ownership of commercial operations, there was one notable addition to the scene. Down a side street, at the other end of the township from the "Big Dog toilet block," was a second toilet block, with a sign above it reading *Tirau's Outhouse*. The external construction was of a style frequently associated with the iconic New Zealand long drop, a toilet consisting of a hole in the ground, often located at the bottom of gardens and protected by sheets of corrugated iron. Outside the toilet block was a corrugated iron figure seated on a toilet pan and reading a fictional newspaper (*Corrugated Courier*). Beside that figure was a further toilet pan on which visitors could sit and have their picture taken (see Figure 3.10). Taking a picture or moving in to read what is written on the mock newspapers,

Figure 3.10 Second Toilet Block, Tirau. *Source:* Photo Credit Diane Johnson.

tourists would inevitably position themselves as voyeurs, appearing to have transgressed a number of generally accepted social boundaries and taking part in the type of bawdy humor that was often associated in the past with seaside postcards.

Above this newly erected toilet block was a corrugated iron native pigeon (*kereru*) of the type that roosts in the local cabbage trees from which the township gets its current name. On the side were a corrugated iron kiwi (New Zealand's most iconic flightless bird) and a corrugated iron possum (an animal introduced by European settlers in the 1950s). The mock newspapers featured articles and advertisements in English relating to Tirau's tourist attractions. Among the headlines was *Tirau Crowned Corrugated Capital of the Universe,* a headline that reinforces the sense of self-mockery that pervades Tirau's tourist-focused semiotoscape. While all of this seemed to contribute in a positive way to the general atmosphere of the township's commercial area, it did nothing to reduce the sense that this was a place almost untouched by the country's indigenous inhabitants.

CONCLUSION

What we see here is an example of landscape as "unwitting autobiography" (Lewis, 1979, p. 121), a creative and imaginative re-working of a rural colonial myth in which artifacts of the dominant culture are re-appropriated and re-shaped (Hall & Jefferson, 1976; Jackson, 1987) in ways that are imbued with an ironic sense of self-recognition and social identity (Stewart & Strathern, 2003, p. 2 & 3).

In reconstructing part of the township's landscape in a creative way, Tirau residents engaged in a re-conceptualization of a type of national identity mythology, one in which New Zealanders are portrayed as an honest, hard-working, self-denigrating, and uncomplicated race of rural dwellers, descendants of European settlers who overcame a hostile environment, beating back the bush to create flourishing farms and making do with whatever was available to them in the process. Nowhere in the original myth was there any acknowledgment of the indigenous people who first tamed the land and successfully cultivated it. These indigenous people have also been largely erased from the re-imagining of that national creation myth in the form of the mythic rural idyll that is contemporary Tirau. The near absence of images of indigenous people from the commercial landscape is reinforced by the almost total absence of any indication of their linguistic heritage. Hence, the particular poignancy of the *lone tino rangatiratanga* (Māori independence) flag visible within the area surveyed.

After all that Māori have achieved since the second half of the twentieth century, it is still possible to erase them symbolically from the landscape, even from a recreated commercially based landscape designed to attract visitors and tourists and even in a context in which Māori have contributed so much to the country's tourist enterprises.

While the creation of a colonial fantasy-scape helped Tirau successfully survive a major economic downturn, the number of commercial outlets for sale in 2016 suggests that the time may have come for a further re-imagining, one in which the role of Māori in the creation of the township is acknowledged. That some re-imagining may be required is further supported by the fact that a private operator who had been leasing an i-SITE which operated from inside the iconic sheepdog information center failed to renew the lease and a tender for its operation gained no interest. At the end of January 2020, therefore, the South Waikato District Council announced that it had been forced to bring the service in-house in order to save it from closure (Kirkeby, 2010).

NOTES

1. The country will be referred to simply as "New Zealand" in subsequent references in this chapter.

2. It was 4.7 million at last reliable census (Statistics New Zealand).

3. This excludes Māori in this case.

4. The next census was delayed due to earthquakes in Christchurch. When it was held, in 2018, there were problems, some of which were caused by an earthquake in Kaikoura, affecting its reliability.

5. The full title is *An Act to Grant a Representative Constitution to the Colony of New Zealand.*

6. The *League of Nations*, now replaced by the *United Nations*, was the first intergovernmental organization whose main aim was to secure world peace.

7. In 1973, Britain, which had been by far the major importer of New Zealand's agricultural products, became a full member of the European Economic Community (EEC). This led to the termination of bilateral agreements with New Zealand. Interim arrangements that initially protected New Zealand from the worst impact had ceased by 1977 and the New Zealand agricultural sector was left heavily reliant on tariff protection and subsidies. These were substantially reduced, or in some cases removed entirely, following the appointment of Roger Douglas as Minister of Finance in New Zealand in 1984 and the introduction of what has come to be known as "Rogernomics," a type of market-led restructuring and deregulation aimed at making the domestic economy more responsive to the consumer. This, together with a shift in the focus of the economy from the productive sector to finance, led to major redundancies and exacerbated the impact of the 1987 stock market crash.

8. Auckland International Airport was opened in 1966. By1985, tourist numbers had reached half a million, with newly developed tourist facilities including farm shows of various kinds (Te Ara: The Encyclopedia of New Zealand (n.d))

9. The Māori name for Hamiliton is *Kirikiriroa*, meaning "long stretch of gravel."

10. The Māori name for Auckland is *Tāmaki Makaurau*, meaning "Tāmaki with a hundred lovers."

11. Taupo is a shortened form of *Taupō-nui-a-Tia*, which translates as "the great cloak of Tia," Tia being an important Māori ancestor.

12. The name Rotorua comes from *Rotorua-nui-a-Kahumatamomoe*, meaning second lake of Kahumatamomoe (uncle of the Māori chief Ihenga).

13. The Māori name for Coromandel Peninsula is *Te Tara-o-te-Ika a Māui*, meaning "the jagged barb of Māui's fish," Māui being a great trickster in Polynesian mythology.

14. The sheep was constructed at the instigation of John Drake, a local landowner.

15. Auckland International Airport was opened in 1966. By 1985, tourist numbers had reached half a million, with newly developed tourist facilities including farm shows of various kinds (Te Ara: The Encyclopedia of New Zealand (n.d)) (see also Note 8 above).

16. August and September 2016.

17. A handle of beer amounts to 59.2 fluid ounces/1.75 liters. Bottles of liquor of this size often had handles attached to make them easier to carry.

18. Handlebar moustaches have long, upward curving extremities and are named for their resemblance to the handlebars of a bicycle.

19. The word "pounamu" can, however, be used appropriately only where the stone used in ornaments is sourced in Aotearoa/New Zealand.

METROPOLITAN FRANCE

PACIFIC COLONIAL EXPANSIONISM

By the end of the second decade of the nineteenth century, having lost most of its earlier colonial conquests (which had centred on North America, the Caribbean, and India), France turned its attention to Africa, Indochina, and the South Pacific. Its approach to colonization was based on the notion of developmental and cultural superiority. This was encapsulated in a speech made in 1884 to the Chamber of Deputies by Jules Ferry (Ferry, 1884)

> Il faut dire ouvertement que les races supérieures ont un droit vis-à-vis des races inférieures. Je répète que les races supérieures ont un droit, parce qu'il y a un devoir pour elles. Elles ont le devoir de civiliser les races inférieures.
>
> [We must say openly that indeed the higher races have a right over the lower races. I repeat, that the superior races have a right because they have a duty. They have the duty to civilize the inferior races.]

Between 1842 and 1901, France established possession of Tahiti, the Tuamotu Archipeligo, New Caledonia, Wallis and Futuna, the Marquesas, the Gambier Islands, Bora Bora, Huahiné, Raiatea, Rapa Nui, Remataru, and Ruratu.

Following World War II, the 1946 Constitution established the French Union (which lasted till 1958), its aim being to assimilate overseas territories into "a greater France . . . blessed by French culture" (Simpson, 2004, p. 286). In reality, this simply meant that although overseas territories and departments had regional assemblies, they had no actual power.

French administrative divisions outside of Europe, amounting to only approximately 1 percent of the area of France's empire at its height, are now almost all either classified as *overseas regions* or *overseas collectives.* In the case of *overseas regions*, French laws and regulations apply in more or less the same way as they do on mainland France (although adaptation in accord with each region's particular needs is possible). *Overseas collectives* are, however, governed by local elected assemblies in association with the French government. These assemblies can make their own laws except in relation to such critical areas as defense, international relations, trade, currency, administration, and the judiciary.

The exceptions to classification as *overseas regions* and *overseas collectives* include French Polynesia and New Caledonia, both of which are in focus here. French Polynesia is classified as an overseas country (*pays d'outre-mer*) and is governed by a Territorial Congress, the French State being represented by a High Commissioner. New Caledonia is classified as a *special collectivity* (*collectivité spéciale*) and has a unique status under the terms of an agreement which granted it political power in relation to key areas such as taxation, labor law, health and hygiene, and foreign trade until a decision is made via referendum as to whether it will become an independent state or revert to being an overseas collectivity (*Accord sur la Nouvelle-Calédonie 1998*; *The Noumea Accord 1998*). Although there has been one such referendum in which the decision was against independence, at least one further referendum will take place in the future.

The situation in which New Caledonia finds itself is not as different from that of other French "outposts" as might at first sight appear to be the case. All of France's former overseas colonies and territories have the right to become independent by invoking Article 53 of the French Constitution, having first consulted the population involved (Maestre & Miclo, 1987, p. 1281). For this reason, political life tends to revolve around the right to independence. In connection with the notion of independence is, however, the ever-present possibility of financial ruin. After all, in 1958 when the *Rassemblement Démocratique des Peuples Tahitiens* (RDPT) in French Polynesia indicated that it favoured secession from France, President De Gaulle announced that, in the case of a vote for independence, all French aid and support would be cut off immediately (Angus, 1995). This was in spite of the damage done by the French Republic to lands and communities in the Pacific.

FRANCE'S ATTITUDE TOWARD THE USE OF LANGUAGES OTHER THAN FRENCH IN ITS TERRITORIES

France has long sought to impose a standardized variety of French in all domains over which it has had authority, often using educational policy as a primary medium of control (Shohamy, 2006, p. 76). Thus, for example, in 1863 a decree was passed banning the teaching of any language other than French in schools (*Décret Guillain 1863/Decree Guillian 1863*). In 1821, all publications in indigenous languages were banned and in 1923 the use of vernaculars in school grounds was forbidden (Mühlhäusler, 2002, p. 188).

In response to the terms of the 1992 Maastricht Treaty upon which the European Union was founded, and its fears that English might in the future become the working language of the Union, France amended its Constitution in such a way as to ensure that the French language was fully recognized as the only official language of the republic (Adamson, 2007). In 1992, however, the Council of Europe proposed a *European Charter for Regional and Minority Languages* (Council of Europe, 1992) which details eight main principles and objectives upon which signatories must base their policies. These include the need for resolute action to promote regional languages, the facilitation and/ or encouragement of the use of such languages in public and private life, and the provision of appropriate forms and means for their teaching and study at all appropriate stages. To date, this Charter has not been ratified by France. However, in 1994, France passed a law whose purpose was to ensure that the French language was given a central position in commercial, educational, employment-related, and public service contexts (La loi Toubon, 1994/The Toubon Law, 1994). In the case of all such activities, written, spoken, and audio-visual, there is a requirement that discourse in languages other than French is accompanied by translation into French, that translation being given equal prominence. In 2000, however, a further law was passed requiring respect for native cultures and languages. This was *La loi d'orientation pour l'outre-mer 2000/Law concerning overseas adaptation 2000.* The most relevant passages (translated into English) are:

Article 33: The State and local communities encourage the respect, protection and maintenance of the knowledge, innovations and practices of indigenous and local communities based on their traditional ways of life and which contribute to the conservation of the natural environment and the sustainable use of the environmental biological diversity.

Article 34: The regional languages used in the communities covered by articles 73 and 74 of the Constitution and in New Caledonia are part of the linguistic heritage of the Nation. They benefit from the strengthening of regional language policies in order to facilitate their use. Articles L. 312-10 and L. 312-11 of the Education Code apply to them.

Article L311-4: School curricula include, at all stages of schooling, lessons designed to make known the diversity and richness of the cultures represented in France. The school, especially through civics lessons, must instil in students respect for the individual, its origins and its differences.

In 2008, a minor change to the French Constitution (*Loi constitutionnelle de modernisation des institutions de la V* Républicque*) involved recognition that regional languages are part of France's heritage,[1] something that is not, however, equivalent to providing them with the status of official languages.

THE FUTURE IMPORTANCE TO FRANCE
OF ITS PACIFIC "POSSESSIONS"

The probable future importance to France of its "possessions" in the Pacific relates in large measure to the Pacific Ocean itself. The *Pacific Islands Forum* (PIF),[2] founded in 1971 (when it was called *The South Pacific Forum*), aims to enhance cooperation among countries and territories of the Pacific. One of its current primary areas of focus is policy concerning the oceans as it relates to climate change, maritime security, fisheries, and biodiversity. In 2016, it was decided to grant New Caledonia and French Polynesia full membership of the Forum. This has raised issues in relation to French involvement in these regions, especially as France, under the terms of the *UN Convention on the Law of the Sea*, controls a vast area ($17,000,000$ km^2) of overseas Exclusive Economic Zone (EEZ)[3] in the Pacific Ocean. France is clearly keenly aware of the significance of this. In fact, Maclellan (2018, §2.3, ¶ 9) has claimed that the concerns of the Kanak and Maohi[4] peoples in the French territories rank relatively low so far as metropolitan France is concerned when compared with its wider strategic interests in the context of China's growing influence in the Indo-Pacific region and its competition for marine resources, including fisheries, deep sea oil and gas, seabed minerals, and marine biodiversity.

NOTES

1. Article 75-1 asserts that regional languages belong to the patrimony of France ("Les langues régionales appartiennent au patrimoine de la France").

2. Membership is Australia, Cook Islands, Federated States of Micronesia, Fiji, French Polynesia, Kiribati, Nauru, New Caledonia, New Zealand, Niue, Palau, Papua New Guinea, Republic of Marshall Islands, Samoa, Solomon Islands, Tonga, Tuvalu, and Vanuatu.

3. EEZ = area of coastal water and seabed within a certain distance of a country's coastline, to which the country claims exclusive rights for fishing, drilling, and other economic activity.

4. Kanak people are native to New Caledonia and Maohi (Mā'ohi) people are native to French Polynesia.

Chapter 4

Assertion and Resistance in the Linguistic Landscape of Kanaky/New Caledonia

INTRODUCTION AND BACKGROUND

Location and Occupation

Kanaky[1]/New Caledonia, with a land area of 18,576 km², is located in the Melanesian region of the southwest Pacific Ocean. Situated south of Vanuatu and approximately 1,210 km east of Australia and 20,000 km from metropolitan France, it has a tropical climate and has, per square kilometer, the richest diversity of flora and fauna in the world. It is made up of la Grande Terre (the main island), les Îles Loyauté (the Loyalty Islands), les Îles Chesterfield (the Chesterfield Islands, located in the Coral Sea), l'Archipel des *Bélep* (the Belep archipelago), l'Île des Pins (the Isle of Pines), and a few remote islets. There are currently three provinces—the North Province, the South Provinces, and the Loyalty Islands Province. Its population is, according to a 2019 census, just under 283,300 of whom approximately 40 percent are of indigenous Kanak descent and just under 30 percent of European descent (mostly French in origin). The remainder are largely from the Wallis and Futuna Islands, Tahiti, Vietnam, Indonesia, and other parts of Asia.

Inhabited since around 1,350 BCE by the Lapida people who are thought to be relatives of modern day Pacific Islanders, the archipelago was sighted in 1744 by the British explorer, Captain Cook, who named it New Caledonia. It was, however, the French who took possession of the archipelago. In 1844, the French naval commander Laferrière and thirteen chiefs signed a treaty which purported to make the lands a French protectorate. However, in order to avoid engaging in hostilities with other Western powers intent on colonizing the region, France did not take full possession of the island until 1853 when Admiral Despointes did so without any further attempt at negotiation except in the case of the nearby Isle of Pines whose chief's consent was sought.

From the mid-1800s, New Caledonia attracted the attention of sandalwood traders and missionaries. It became a French penal colony from 1864 until 1897 during which time approximately 22,000 criminals and political prisoners were transported there. Later (from the early 1840s until 1904), it became a source of slaves to work on sugar plantations, mainly in Australia. When, in 1864, the discovery of nickel led to the establishment of mines, the indigenous population was not permitted to participate in the resulting economic activity and was largely relegated to reservations covering only 10 percent of their ancestral lands. The conditions in these reservations worsened considerably as a result of the severity of the colonial response to a Kanak uprising in 1878. Kanaks were no longer permitted to leave reservations without official permission and the *pilou-pilou* ceremonies which brought people from different areas together ceased, as did the cultural practices associated with them. All of this, combined with introduced diseases, had a disastrous impact on Kanak numbers, with a reduction of approximately 80 percent between the time of Cook's arrival and the official census of 1921when it seemed that the indigenous population might become extinct (Ammann, 1997, p. 6; Rouvray, 1946, p. 1212).

In 1931, a group of Kanak people attended a Colonial Exhibition at Vincennes in Paris where they were exhibited as cannibals (Ammann, 1997, p. 7). Attitudes, however, began to change shortly thereafter. In March 1942, during World War II, New Caledonia became an Allied base, with the main South Pacific Fleet of the U.S. Navy moving to its capital city, Noumea,[2] between 1942 and 1943. In 1946, New Caledonia was given the status of French overseas territory. By 1953, French citizenship had been granted to people of all ethnicities. Around that time, true Kanak songs and dances began to be tolerated. By the late 1960s, overseas protest movements, particularly in France, began to have an impact on the Kanak people. A Kanak independence movement, led by Jean-Marie Tjibaou, began to insist on the need for political independence coupled with the living expression of Kanak culture.

THE INDIGENOUS PEOPLE: CULTURE, LANGUAGE, POVERTY, AND ALIENATION

So far as traditional Kanak society and custom are concerned, there is a strong emphasis on clan affiliation, with a distinction between land and sea clans being based on location and traditional occupation types. Family groups, which generally live on a husband's clan site, include several generations.

The society is patrilineal, with land being passed from father to son. While men are dominant in public speaking, silence and discretion are highly valued in other contexts. Women are expected to maintain spatial distance from men, remaining silent or using special politeness terms except in certain familiar and/or familial contexts. Gift giving and oratory mark initial encounters with strangers who are closely observed and judged on the basis of their behavior. While officially embracing Christianity, contemporary Kanaks may also subscribe to traditional beliefs, which involve supernatural protection, the enduring presence of ancestors, and a subaqueous after life. Sickness is often considered to be the result of sorcery or the vengeance of disrespected ancestors and may be treated, sometimes now in combination with Western medicine, with plant-based remedies and incantations administered by special healers (Ramsay, 2011).

In addition to being involved in wood carving, sculpting, painting, basket weaving, and music-making, Kanaks have vast resources of oral literature, including poetry, myths, epics, tales, and historical accounts, and there are now some literary texts available in Kanak languages. There have, however, been major cultural losses.

Currently, approximately 15 percent of New Caledonia's gross domestic product (GDP) is made up of financial support from France. However, although it has little arable land and imports around one fifth of its food, New Caledonia does have over 10 percent of the world's nickel resource. This, in spite of price volatility, is a major source of income and employment. Another important source of income is hospitality and tourism. New Caledonia's unemployment rate fell from 14.6 percent in 2016 to 11.6 percent the following year. As at mid-2019, it had, however, risen again and was about 50 percent higher for Kanaks than it was for other ethnic groups.

James Anaya, Special Rapporteur on the rights of indigenous peoples, was invited by France to review the Kanak situation. He noted in 2011 that Kanaks were experiencing poor levels of educational attainment, employment, and health as well as being over-represented in Government-subsidized housing, urban poverty, and exposure to land and water pollution. He also observed that a disproportionate number were living in poverty, with around 8,000 existing in housing settlements in Noumea that lacked access to municipal water, electricity, and sewage services. Furthermore, at least 90 percent of those in prison were of Kanak descent and many of them were under the age of twenty-five (Anaya, 2011). As recorded in a 36th parallel risk assessment report (Buchanan, 2014, ¶ 4):

> New Caledonia is a classic instance of what is known as a "dual society." The majority of the population, including the national élite, lives in relatively modernized urban areas in and around Nouméa and is connected to the globalized

political economy via technological, cultural, entrepreneurial and social means. The minority, located in the North and Loyalty Islands, live in largely pre-modern rural conditions with traditional social hierarchies and are only casually connected to the outside world via technology, tourism and relatively limited economic enterprise.

LANGUAGE

The French language, either the standardized metropolitan variety or, more commonly, a New Caledonian variety, is spoken throughout the archipelago, even on remote islands, but with varying degrees of proficiency. Tayo, a French creole, is also spoken, mainly in rural areas. There are, in addition, twenty-eight surviving Kanak languages. Inter-generational transmission of these Kanak languages is necessarily patchy in view, in part, of the general drift to the south, and some are seriously endangered. In the 2009 edition of UNESCO's *Atlas of Endangered Languages*, eighteen Kanak languages were listed as endangered, with five of these listed as critical.

It was not until 1984 that the *Décret Guillain*, banning the teaching of languages other than French in schools, was rescinded, not until 1998 that the *Nouméa Accord* put forward a legal argument for the use of Kanak languages and not until 2005 that congress introduced the teaching of Kanak and Oceanic languages and culture into official programs in Primary Schools.

Although there has been some optional teaching of Kanak languages in schools since 2006, that teaching has been patchy and sporadic and limited availability of teachers and teaching resources means that children are sometimes taught Kanak languages that are not those of their own ancestors. In addition, although some children's readers in Kanak languages are now available,[3] it is unclear what their readership is intended to be given that they appear not to be related to school curricula or to have been designed with input from applied linguists who are familiar with children's reading development (Sallabank, 2014).

Four Kanak languages are taught to Bachelor's degree level at the University of New Caledonia which was founded in 1993. There is, in addition, now a Kanak Language Academy, founded in 2007, which is charged with protecting and developing Kanak languages and dialects as well as developing and/or perfecting written forms of these languages.

None of this appears, however, to be making serious inroads in the context of an ideological tradition which presupposes the superiority of the French language (Salaün, 2007).

FIGHTING BACK

In the late 1960s, with the nickel sector booming, more than 8,000 citizens from metropolitan France moved to New Caledonia along with several thousand migrants from other French Pacific territories (Kowasch, 2010). Meanwhile, the "Billotte laws" of 1969 transferred the New Caledonian district administration back to France and ensured that nickel mining licenses were reserved to the French State. At the beginning of the 1970s, however, the price of nickel on the world market fell, leading to a severe economic downturn in New Caledonia. In 1975, a number of Kanak organizations formed a coordinating committee for Kanak independence (Leblic, 2003), and in 1984 the national Parliament voted in favor of internal self-governance for five years followed by an independence referendum. In spite of this, there was no acknowledgment of the Kanak call for the right to self-determination. It was largely this that provided the motivation for a reorganization of the Kanak independence movement leading to the formation of the *Kanak and Socialist National Liberation Front (Front de Libération Nationale Kanak et Socialiste: FLNKS)* which boycotted the 1984 elections and called for land reclamation and cultural recognition (Chappell, 2013).

In November of 1984, violent clashes broke out between the pro-independence Kanaks and Europeans who opposed independence. As a result, France declared a state of emergency which lasted for six months. Outbursts of violence were intensified in 1987 after a center-right government, elected in France in March 1986, began eroding arrangements for Kanak sovereignty and redistributing land in such a way as to reduce Kanak ownership to less than one third of what it had been under the socialist administration. Attempts to engage in a peace and reconciliation process were disrupted in 1988 when Kanak separatists attacked a police station and took twenty-seven hostages. The French government retaliated, resulting in the death of nineteen Kanaks. This was a major turning point. That year, separatists and loyalists agreed that there would be a decade of Kanak development, during which the issue of independence would not be raised (*Accords de Matignon* 1988/The Matignon Agreements). Even so, Kanak development continued to be managed by the colonial administration. The main beneficiary of development expenditure was the province in which 70 percent of the European and immigrant population is located. This led to an intensification of a rural exodus which was already representing a threat to the survival of Kanak identities (Winslow, 1991).

Ten years after the signing of The Matignon Agreements, it was decided that a referendum would be held in 2018 to determine whether New Caledonia would remain as a special collectivity of France (with semi-autonomous status) or regain its independence (*L'accord de Nouméa 1998*/The Noumea

Accord 1998).[4] The referendum turnout was 81 percent of the 174,995 people who were eligible to vote. Of these, just under 57 percent voted against independence. There was, however, a clear ethnic divide in the voting, with a very strong vote in favor of independence in areas of high Kanak occupancy. Emmanuel Macron, President of France, arrived in Noumea just one hour after the official result was announced. In his address, he claimed that the result indicated confidence in the French republic and its values and was a sign of pride in being French.

The referendum result led to renewed confidence among Kanak liberationists and the Kanak liberation flag was in evidence across the archipelago (Zweifel, 2018). The *Nouméa Accord* provided for the possibility of further referenda in 2020 and 2022 should the initial vote be against independence. The population profile indicates that there are likely to be a higher proportion of Kanak voters in any future independence referenda as more young Kanaks reach voting age.

EXPLORING THE LINGUISTIC LANDSCAPE: THE SITES

The foci of the case studies discussed here are the *Jean-Marie Tjibaou* Cultural *Center* (*Centre Culturel Tjibaou*) and the *Federation of Lay Works* (*Fédération des Oeuvres Laïques—FOL*), two locations which are in many ways diametrically opposed. The first is housed in a building which has been described as being "unsurpassed in the Pacific for its architectural splendor" (Jolly, 2001, p. 434); the second is an abandoned concrete building due for demolition.

The Jean-Marie Tjibaou *Cultural* Center
(*Centre Culturel Tjibaou: CCT*)

The *Jean-Marie Tjibaou* Cultural *Center,* located on the outskirts of Noumea (*see Figure 4.1*), was formally inaugurated in May 1998, the day before the signing of the *Noumea Accord*. It houses the *Agency for the Development of Kanak Culture* (*Agence pour le développement de la culture Kanak*: ADCK). The building was designed by the Italian architect Renzo Piano, assisted by Alban Bensa, a French anthropologist specializing in Kanak culture. The design, intended to be reminiscent of aspects of Kanak villages, is made up of an interconnected series of ten stylized "chiefly huts" which are constructed of stainless steel and iroko, an African rot-resistant timber. Along the pathway from the car park to the entrance are plants from various regions of the archipelago. Together, these represent the myth of the creation of the first human: the founding hero, *Téâ Kanaké*. The Center's Mission includes

Figure 4.1 Jean-Marie Tjibaou Cultural Centre, Noumea, New Caledonia. *Source:* Photo Credit Diane Johnson.

promoting Kanak linguistic and archaeological heritage, supporting Kanak contemporary forms of expression, especially in the field of handcraft, broadcasting technology and art, developing cross regional interaction, especially in the South Pacific, and planning courses of study (The Tjibaou Cultural Center and ADCK, n.d.).

Following the interim peace accord recorded in the Matignon Agreements, arrangements were made for the establishment of this Center. Mitterrand, President of France at the time, believed that it would stand, like the Pomidou Center (*Centre Georges Pompidou*) in Paris, as a testament to the contemporary significance of the French republic. The intention was that it would be the first of a group of "Great Projects of the Republic," to be invested in or built outside of France (Main, 1998, p. 9).

The Kanak leader of the pro-independence *Union Calédonienne* party, Jean-Marie Tjibaou, had asked the French government to build a center of this type. When he was assassinated in 1989 after signing the precursor to the *Noumea Accord* (*Accords de Matignon-Oudinot 1988*/*Matignon-Oudinot Accords* 1988), it was decided to name the center after him. Its focus on contemporary works, including its inclusion of very few art objects, is often justified in relation to Tjibaou's insistence on the importance of ensuring a forward-looking rather than static or backward-looking future for Kanaks. Thus, for example, Message, Professor of Public Humanities at the Australian National University, observes that The Center's approach can be deemed to be "[a]ppropriate to Tjibaou's dream for Kanak culture to resist becoming caught in the past or rendered as static" (Message, 2006, p. 16).[5] She adds that while it has a well-resourced library and digital catalog that facilitate access to, and preservation of, Kanak cultural heritage, it also promotes engagement by rural Kanak communities through outreach programs that include artists' workshops and traveling educational kits (p. 10). In addition, she maintains that it has "many of the key components and features that have become identified with a shift in the way that museums are conceptualized in the Western world" (p. 9). Finally, she argues that "[e]xpanding its focus [to include non-Kanak Oceanian exhibits] has meant it can highlight the intersections and cross-cultural dialogue that have historically occurred between communities and cultural forms in New Caledonia" (p. 21).

In an article published in *The Contemporary Pacific*, Margaret Jolly (2001, p. 434) describes the Center in the following terms:

> The Tjibaou Cultural Centre is unsurpassed in the Pacific for its architectural splendour and its expensive high-tech virtuosity. It sustains a singular stress on contemporary Pacific arts rather than the curating and display of older objects. . . . There are about thirty older artefacts in the Bwenaado house (mainly masks, houseposts, and roof sculptures on loan from European museums), but most older Kanak artefacts are still housed in the Territorial Museum of New Caledonia in town. The emphasis . . . is rather on contemporary works by named artists in both indigenous and introduced genres.

Comparing the monumental splendor of the Tjibaou Cultural Center with the simplicity of a low key forest-based cultural center on Loyalty island, Losche (2003, p. 81) notes that Emmanuel Kasarhérou, a former cultural director of the CCT, has drawn attention to the fact that although the CCT is reminiscent of Kanak houses, it nevertheless aspires to architectural modernism, arguing that this gives it a sense of sense of incompleteness that acts as a reminder that "Kanak culture itself is not static but is always open to change" (Kasarhérou quoted in Losche, 2003, p. 81). Peter Brown, on the other hand, in a review of a book by Alban Bensa,[6] notes that the reality, notwithstanding claims to democratic openness, is that this is a building that was authorized, commissioned, approved and financed by a Western European state, one that, at a symbolic level, "updates" Kanak huts in a way that makes them appear to be more consistent with European notions of modernity and progress (Brown, 2002, p. 283). Furthermore, writing about the relationship between architectural monuments and the media campaigns that may be constructed to influence their interpretation, Lawrence Vale notes that the reporting surrounding the Center risks privileging a forward-looking focus that, when accompanied by a lack of critical analysis, makes only "politically useful" links to the past (Vale, 1999, p. 391).

In an attempt to explain a low level of involvement of Kanak people in the Center, Emmanuel Kasarhérou (1992, p. 166) has argued as follows:

[An] explanation of our difficulties in attracting Kanak visitors is their fear of entering a place where artefacts of the past are displayed. They feel as if they were entering a cemetery where devils live. The matter however must not be forced, attitudes will change gradually. The only thing to do is to explain why it is important for the future of our cultures to have a museum. We must explain why museums did not exist in the past and why they are important nowadays.

There are very different perspectives on this issue. Thus, for example, Anne Pitoiset has argued that the underwhelming support by Kanaks for the Center may relate to the fact that it lacks an historical perspective and, as a result, risks denying the realities of colonization (Pitoiset, 2002, p. 145). In connection with this, it is interesting to note that Rangiiria Hedley, a former curator and conservator of *taonga Maori* [Maori treasures], has argued that the management and interpretation of tribal treasures of all kinds, treasures which should not be separated from the stories that are an essential part of their meaning and purpose, should be in the hands of those to whom they belong (Hedley, 2004, p. 50). The real reasons for the low level of participation by Kanak people in the Center may be rather different and rather more nuanced than Kasarhérou would allow, relating, in particular, to their experiences of past colonial practices and promises.

The Federation of Lay Works (*Fédération des Oeuvres Laïques—FOL*)

The *Federation of Lay Works* building is located in the center of Noumea on top of a very steep hill from which there are excellent views of the city and harbor. Now that the iconic Noumea "Tchou Tchou Train," a long train-shaped motorized vehicle which used to take visitors around the city, no longer visits the FOL lookout point, it can be approached only by car or by climbing approximately 100 steps set into the hillside. The FOL building was intended as part of a movement, well-known in France, whose aim is to promote equal secular educational opportunities in the realms of sport, culture, and peace, bringing together individual efforts under one roof. It was in the past a vibrant hub of cultural activities, hosting gatherings of different types, including exhibitions and concerts.[7] Because of its location near the center of the city, it was readily accessible and became a meeting place for peoples of all ethnicities, particularly the young. In February 2011, however, Cyclone

Vania blew the roof off the building and deterioration set in. There was much discussion about the future of the building but no action was taken. A few isolated instances of graffito soon became many until the exterior of the building was almost totally covered, and then repeatedly re-covered, producing an ever-changing exterior. Visitors who had initially come to view the city and harbor from this lookout point began to come also to view the graffiti. Messages left online by visitors suggest that while some interpreted these graffiti as works of street art, others felt considerable distaste for what they saw as desecration of the building (Tripadvisor New Zealand: Noumea, n.d.). On July 13th, 2018, the interior of the building was set on fire and thereafter roped off and on April 16th, 2019, it was announced that this emblematic building would be demolished.

Exploring the Linguistic Landscape of the Federation of Lay Works

My last visit to the *Federation of Lay Works* (FOL) was in June 2019. It was then that I viewed the signs and took the photographs of the images and writing on the exterior of the building that are reported on and/or reproduced here.

The term "*graffiti*" is used here as a generic term, that is, it is used in a way that includes writings or drawings, generally (but not always) unsanctioned and now mainly made with paint or marker pen (sometimes stenciled), on a wall or other surface in public view. All graffiti, irrespective of the intent of those responsible for them, can be considered to be subversive in the sense that they are likely to undermine, unsettle or destabilize the *status quo* or some aspect or aspects of it. This includes graffiti that are simply the expression of some form of exuberance, graffiti that are intended as identity markers of individuals or gangs (which often take the form of *tags* or stylized signatures), and graffiti that are intended to convey personal or political messages, either positive or negative (including those that may be considered to be obscene, profane and/or defamatory).

When I last visited the FOL, years of superimposition, graffiti upon graffiti, had resulted in a situation in which it was difficult, generally impossible, to determine where one graffito ended and another began. It was, therefore, impossible to undertake any form of quantitative analysis. Nevertheless, it *was* possible to determine that the vast majority were in the form of tags in Roman alphabetic script, interspersed with a few drawings and even fewer comprehensible word-based messages. The most immediately obvious word-based graffito, one whose author/s clearly intended that it should not disappear into the background or be covered by other graffiti, was written in French in very large orange capital letters placed higher than most of the other graffiti. It took the form of an ambiguous directive: RÊVONS LA FOL

Figure 4.2   First Impression of Graffiti on the Abandoned FOL Building in Noumea.
Source: Photo Credit Diane Johnson.

(see *Figure 4.2*). While FOL is clearly an acronym for the name of the building, *Fédération des Oeuvres Laïques*, "la fol" also translates as "the crazy"
or "the idiotic." Thus, while this message may be interpreted by some as
involving simple nostalgia (Dream/Let's dream of the FOL), it may also be
interpreted as a type of memorial protest (Dream/Let's dream of the crazi-
ness/idiocy), a reminder, perhaps, of the fact that the then current situation
(the contrast between the FOL past and present) could have been avoided
were it not for the crazy/ idiotic failure on the part of those who had the power
to save this important cultural resource but failed to do so. This is, of course,
something that could also be applied symbolically to the failure of France
to acknowledge and respond appropriately and promptly to the impact of
its colonial agenda on Kanak society, reducing it to a state of near collapse,
similar to that of the FOL. Interestingly, this graffito is an alteration of one
that appeared several years ago, then reading SAUVONS LA FOL (Save/
Let's Save the FOL). A picture of the original graffito was accompanied in
an online posting in 2014 (Rénovation de la FOL, 2014) by a message, part
of which is printed below:

Dans une lettre datant du début de la semaine, le président de la province Sud,
Philippe Michel, réaffirme à la Fédération des œuvres laïques de Nouvelle-
Calédonie (FOL) le soutien de l'institution dans le projet de rénovation du centre culturel dit de *"la colline."* Il y émet toutefois plusieurs conditions, estimant
le *"risque financier considerable pour la province."*

[In a letter at the beginning of the week, the president of the southern province, Philippe Michel, reaffirms the Federation of New Caledonia Secular Works (FOL) institutional support for the renovation of the cultural center, "the hill." It does however, make several conditions, estimating that there would be considerable financial risk for the province].

In connection with this, it is relevant to note that less than two decades earlier the CCT, a building that had cost France 320 million francs, had been officially opened (Murphy, 2002, p.81).[8]

Apart from tags, I could decipher, in full, only five other word-based graffiti (three in English; two in French). These are reproduced below with the original upper and lower case lettering retained.

The three English graffiti were "HAPPY BIRTHDAY ZEETOON," "SLOW," and "BIG UP LA DOSE," and the last of these (see Figure 4.3 below)[9] is, like the large graffito discussed above, ambiguous. "Big up" is a Jamaican term of encouragement or support, a term that can also be used as a directive (to increase) and "da" is Jamaican creole for "the" or "this." The word "dose" may simply refer to one intake of something. Alternatively, it may refer to an STD (sexually transmitted disease) or, indeed, anything particularly unpleasant (Dere, L'A., 2012). Bearing all this in mind, one possible interpretation of this sign is "increase the anti/opposition," an interpretation that makes sense in the context of widespread anger in New Caledonia at the decision not to rebuild the FOL. It also makes sense in

Figure 4.3 Graffiti on the Abandoned FOL Building in Noumea. *Source:* Photo Credit Diane Johnson.

relation to the impact that reggae, and the hip hop movement it inspired, have had on anti-colonial and anti-racist counterculture movements among Kanaks in New Caledonia (Webb & Webb-Gannon, 2018). However, it is relevant to note that BIG UP is also the name of an American film company whose productions include outdoor adventure films, television shows, and commercials, often involving climbing. Indeed, the company was awarded a Sports Emmy for camera work associated with a segment on Chris Sharma's first ascent of Es Pontas, in Mallorca. The fact that this graffito appeared very high up on the wall of the FOL, in a position that could not be reached by someone standing on the ground, supports the argument that some word-play signaling the difficulty of achieving a desirable outcome may have been intended.

The two graffiti in French were "Joyeux Anniversaire" and "La VICTORE [sic] est belle!!!" (see Figure 4.4 below). The second of these is a common misquotation of the title of a book by Michel Malinovsky—*Seule la victoire est jolie* (Only victory is good/ enjoyable), a title, generally interpreted as being ironic, which refers to the fact that Malinovski is best known for coming second in the *Route du Rhum*, a singlehanded transatlantic yacht race. He completed the course ninety-eight seconds behind the winner after a race lasting

Figure 4.4   A Graffito High up on the Wall of the Abandoned FOL Building in Noumea.
Source: Photo Credit Diane Johnson.

twenty-three days. The fact that the desired victory—saving the FOL—was no longer possible, but had seemed as if it might be until very recently, supports this interpretation. It is an interpretation that is further supported by the fact that the graffito would almost certainly have disappeared into the mass of others had it not been a comparatively recent one, that is, one that is likely to have appeared after the announcement that the FOL building would not be saved.

In addition to the word-based graffiti referred to above, there were three rectangular shaped signs, each of which contained writing in French that I could decipher only in part. In only one case was it possible to guess what the message may have been. That one is visible, with a patterned border on both sides, in Figure 4.3 above. It seemed to me that one letter had been obliterated and that that letter was 'M'. With that letter inserted/restored, the sign would read as follows:

Te es de Maré mais tu n'as pas l'accent!
VALEURS KANAK
TRADITION/ CULTURE

This can be roughly translated into English as:

You are from Maré [the second largest of the Loyalty Islands] but you don't
    sound as if you are
KANAK VALUES
TRADITION/ CULTURE]

I discovered later that the missing letter was in fact "M." This, and the other rectangular signs that were still partially visible were originally part of a poster display that was the outcome of a student assignment. The students, mostly Kanak, were studying for a Bachelor's degree at the University of New Caledonia and were asked to create posters illustrating some of the ways in which they had been subjected to a type of low-level linguistically based abuse. While the statement above may have been intended as a compliment, it would, in the context of contemporary New Caledonian society, be much more likely to be interpreted by the recipient as being indicative of the fact that the speaker had generally low expectations in relation to the standard of the French spoken by Kanaks.

The originals of the posters that were part of the assignment, together with a discussion of the project, is available in an article published in *Palabre* [Palaver] (Razafi & Wacalie, 2018, pp. 46–49).

Overall, of the seven word-based graffiti that were not simple tags that I was able to decipher, three were in English, four in French. None was in a Kanak language although one clearly involved a distinctly Kanak protest. Of the remaining six, three (two taking the form of directives) appeared to involve protest concerning the fate of the FOL, with ambiguity and/or irony appearing to characterize all of them.

Exploring the linguistic landscape of the Tjibaou *Cultural* Center

The Center buildings are made up of 10 units/ hut pavilions of different sizes, referred to as "cases" (houses). Each of these is intended to be representative of a Kanak hut. These buildings, linked by covered walkways, are arranged into three clusters, each representing a Kanak village. In each cluster, one of the buildings, representing a chiefly hut, is taller than the others. In the interior of each building is a number of rooms, each having a different function. In the first cluster, the emphasis is on exhibitions, with a permanent exhibition at the center. There is also a theater and a sunken auditorium. The second cluster houses offices for curators, administrative staff, and so on. These are fronted by a multimedia library and conference halls. The third cluster, located slightly apart from the visitor area, is devoted to creative activities such as dance, painting, sculpture, and music. It includes studios and a teaching center where children can learn local arts and crafts. The Center buildings are surrounded by gardens of native plants bordering a pathway that progresses symbolically through five stages in the tale of the first man, Téâ Kanaké, as recorded in Kanak creation legends.

As in the case of the FOL, my last visit to the *Tjibaou* Cultural *Centre* (CCT) was in June 2019 and it was then that I viewed the signs that are discussed here.

Two signs were immediately apparent on arrival at the Center. One was to the side of the ticket booth; the other was above it. The first, naming the Center and giving opening and closing times, was largely in French and English, the French preceding the English and in larger print. At the top, however, the name of the Center (Tjibaou) appeared in two versions. On the right hand side, the French words *centre culturel* (cultural center) appeared; on the left hand side, the words *ngan jila* appeared. These are the words for "cultural center" in jawe, a Kanak language spoken by members of Jean Tjibaou's tribe in the Northern province of Grande Terre (see Figure 4.5).

The second sign (see Figure 4.6), placed immediately above the reception desk/ticket office, included words in French (at the top), English (in the middle), and Japanese (at the bottom). The French and Japanese conveyed approximately the same informative content. The English, however, included no translation of *billetterie* (ticket office). This, combined with the fact that the function of the information desk/ticketing office is evident at a glance, suggests that the reason for including all three languages (the three spoken by the majority of visitors to the Center) has more to do with publicity and marketing than it does with information sharing.

Figure 4.5   Sign to the Right of the Entrance to the Tjibaou Cultural Centre. *Source:* Photo Credit Diane Johnson.

These two signs set the tone for the other signage on the way to the buildings, in the buildings themselves and in the corridors linking the buildings. The only words on signs that were in Kanak languages that I could see as a visitor to the Center were to do with naming. The one or two-word names of houses, rooms, and some exhibitions (generally permanent features of the Center) were drawn from Kanak languages. Thus, for example, the nomenclature for cases/houses and rooms as recorded on a directional sign in the grounds was:

Bwénaado; Jinu; Kanaké; Pérui; Ngan Vhalik; Mwà Véénemi; Umatë; Mâlep; Eman; Vinimoï
   Bérétara; Kavitara; Komwi

On site, there was rarely any indication that I could detect of the meanings of the words in Kanak languages or any indication of the particular languages from which they were drawn.[10] One exception was a sign advertising an exhibition entitled *Pèmöru Ko* in which there is an explanation of the tile and its linguistic origin in French following the heading.

Wherever text of more than one or two words was in evidence, even where that text introduced Kanak artists and/or explained their work, that text was

Figure 4.6 Sign above Reception/Ticketing Office at the Entrance to the Tjibaou Cultural Centre. *Source:* Photo Credit Diane Johnson.

in French only, in a combination French, and English, or in a combination of French, English, and Japanese. This was, however, sometimes accompanied by headings in a Kanak language.

During my visit to the Center, the café was closed, there were no guided tours, and none of the staff members I saw, with one exception—a middle aged woman cleaning the stairs—appeared to be of Kanak ethnicity. The only sounds, apart from natural ones such as birdsong, came from the French commentary accompanying a video of Kanak men engaged in traditional building. And yet, it would have been a very simple matter to flood the building with recorded Kanak voices, with ever-changing song and talk in Kanak languages. It would have been possible also to have signs, constantly revolving and changing, that displayed writing in a range of Kanak languages. It might even have been possible to arrange for visitors to be welcomed and hosted by Kanak staff and to have Kanak artists working on some of their crafts in public spaces in the buildings.

CONCLUSION

Rising high above the surrounding countryside 8 km from the center of Noumea stands the CCT, an impressive symbol of French magnificence. When I visited in June 2019, its linguistic landscape, which included only the occasional concession to Kanak languages in the form of one-or-two-word labels, seemed to highlight the dominance of three of the world's major cultures while reinforcing, notwithstanding the building's avowed function, the subordination of indigeneity. In stark contrast, in the very heart of the city of Noumea stood the FOL—empty, neglected and awaiting demolition, a symbol of desolation, broken promises and despair, a symbol, ultimately, of the absence of that hegemonic transformation that had seemed possible just two decades earlier. Years of superimposition, graffiti upon graffiti, had rendered most of the writing on the walls incomprehensible. The original large printed plea—SAUVONS LA FOL—was nothing more than a distant memory, its replacement—RÊVONS LA FOL—communicating a combined sense of defeat and anger. It should be remembered, however, that the existing hegemony is always open to reconfiguration. A further referendum on independence may take place in the near future.

NOTES

1. This term is preferred to "New Caledonia" by pro-independence groups (Nēaoutyine, 2006). They refer to the archipelago as "kanaky" and to themselves as "kanak," these words being derived from the word for "man" or "human being" in Hawaiian and some other related languages (Sallabank, 2015, p. 33). Those associated with the political independence movement prefer to spell these words without an initial capital letter, the bislama spelling (Ammann, 1997). I have, however, used an initial capital here in line with the tradition in English to do so in the case of all countries and peoples.

2. Noumea is spelt without an accent except where the co-text is French rather than English or where a quotation includes the version with an accent.

3. One example is Ouetcho and Derton (2012), *Nyùwâxè, l'igname amè* [Bitter yam]. Nouvelle-Calédonie: ADCK—centre culturel Tjibaou.

4. The Noumea Accord recognized the fact that colonization had undermined the dignity of the Kanak people and compromised their identity (Faberon & Postic, 2004).

5. Material of relevance to Jean Marie Tjibaou's life is located in the Mâlep House, the word *mâlep* meaning "living" in the *yâlayu* language.

6. Alban Bensa is a French anthropologist and specialist on New Caledonia and Kanak culture.

7. In the 1980s, when I lived and worked in Noumea, I took part in a competition held there. I was the only non-Kanak member of a group of musicians. As winners of the competition, we received money and a small Kanak carved statue. The Kanak members of the group gifted the statue, that of a Kanak warrior, to me and it remains as an inspiration and caution in relation to any work I do that relates to indigenous rights and values.

8. In addition, it seems unlikely that a public building of this type was not covered by natural disaster insurance.

9. The words that can be seen on a rectangular sign above this graffito are discussed below.

10. It may be that tour guides were able to communicate this information but there were no tours during my visit. I did, however, find information online about the names listed above together with translations into French. I have provided that information (but with translations into English) below.

Case names: Bwénaado (Language: cèmuhî; Rough translation: customary gathering); Jinu (Languages: jawe, pije, fwâi, nemi; Rough translation: mind/ spirit); Kanaké (Language: paicî; Rough translation: man/person); Pérui (Language: nenemwâ; Rough translation: encounter); Ngan Vhalik (Language: pije; Rough translation: house of speech/debating house); Mwà Véénemi (Language: drubea; Rough translation: house of speech/debating house); Umatë (Language: drehu; Rough translation: the storage place for yams); Mâlep (Language: yâlayu; Rough translation: live/ living); Eman (Language: nengone; Rough translation: palaver); Vinimoï (Language: ajïe; Rough translation: Telling stories to children).

Room names: Bérétara (Language: xârâcùù; Rough meaning: look/ admire); Kavitara (Language: ajië; Rough translation: threshold sculpture); Komwi (Language: nemi: Rough translation: show/exhibit).

Chapter 5

Pape'ete

A City at Sea

LOCATION, TOPOGRAPHY, CLIMATE, POPULATION, FLORA, AND FAUNA

Te Ao Mā'ohi is now commonly referred to as French Polynesia (since 1957). It is a country made up of 118 islands and atolls with a total land mass of just over 4,000 km² spread over more than 2,000 km in the South Pacific Ocean. It is approximately 3,000 km south of Hawai'i and half way between New Zealand to the west and South America to the east. It is over 1,700 km from metropolitan France. There are five island groups: the *Tuāmotu Archipelago*; the *Gambier Islands*; the *Marquesas Islands*; the *Austral Islands*; and the *Society Islands* (made up of the *Windward Islands* and the *Leeward Islands*). Among the islands and atolls that make up French Polynesia, sixty-seven are inhabited. The whole area is currently referred to by the French Republic as an overseas country (*pays d'outre-mer*) of France.

The largest island, Tahiti, is located in the *Windward group* of the *Society Islands*. It is made up of two ancient volcanic cones—*Tahiti Nui* and *Tahiti Iti*—which are connected by the *Isthmus of Taravao*. With a total land area of 1,043 km², Tahiti makes up a large part of the total land area of French Polynesia. It is also home to almost three quarters of the population of French Polynesia, which, according to a 2017 census, is just over 280,000 (*Recensement de la population,* 2017). Tahiti is the location of the capital, Pape'ete, which is home to almost half of the total population of French Polynesia. Polynesians make up approximately 70 percent of the population of the island of Tahiti, the remainder being made up largely of Europeans, Chinese, and people of mixed heritage. Most of those from metropolitan France live in Pape'ete and its suburbs.

The climate of French Polynesia is temperate, with two seasons—humid (from November to March) and cool and dry (from April to October). The marine wildlife includes multi-colored coral, tiger and gray sharks, manta rays, giant turtles, parrotfish, angelfish, clown fish, butterfly fish, barracudas, and dolphins. Some of the many species of fish unique to French Polynesia include Marquesan Parrotfish and Yellow-belly Damsels. There are over 100 bird species, including lorikeets, pigeons, monarch binds, doves, and sand-pipers. Butterflies, moths, weevils, and cicadas are also plentiful.

It seems likely that the ancestors of the Polynesian settlers (the Mā'ohi) inhabited Sāmoa around 800 BCE and colonized the central Society Islands between 1025 and 1120 CE, dispersing from there to New Zealand, Hawai'i, Rapa Nui, and other locations. Large chieftainships were formed on Tahiti, Bora-Bora and Ra'iātea, on the last of which the most sacred shrine was located (Wilmshurst et al., 2011).

The first Europeans to site Tahiti may have been Spaniards (Juan Fernández in 1576-1577 and Pedro Fernandes de Queirós in 1606). It was not, however, until the period between the Seven Years' War and the American Revolutionary War (1763–1765) that serious European inroads were made into the area. In 1767, Tahiti was visited by a British sea captain, Samuel Wallis. The following year, and just before a visit by the Frenchman Louis-Antoine de Bougainville, a vicious war to determine who would be paramount chief began. In spite of the fact that that war continued after de Bougainville's visit, he portrayed Tahiti as a Polynesian paradise. A more unsentimental version of Tahiti and Tahitian society was, however, presented by British sea captain James Cook who visited Tahiti in 1769,[1] 1772, and 1773, spending some time during the first visit meeting clan chiefs and gathering information about the islands and their inhabitants. In 1772 and again in 1773, the Viceroy of Peru sent expeditions under the command of Domingo de Bonechea to colonize the islands.[2] Visiting again in 1774, a Peruvian expedition left two friars in charge of the Spanish mission. That mission was, however, abandoned in 1775 due to Polynesian resistance (Delaney, 2010).

In 1778, HMS *Bounty*, under the command of Captain William Bligh, landed in Tahiti, its mission being to collect Tahitian breadfruit seedlings to transport to the Caribbean.[3] After remaining there for several months, the crew set out again. Three weeks' later, however, they followed Fletcher Christian in a mutiny. A group of the mutineers returned to settle in Tahiti, providing chief Tū with arms and becoming mercenaries in the battles that resulted in his eventual establishment as the first king of all of Tahiti (in 1790) in what came to be known as the Pōmare Dynasty.

In the 1790s, whalers began landing at Tahiti, as did merchants from Australia's penal colonies. The introduction of weapons and alcohol, together with the spread of introduced ailments (such as dysentery, smallpox, scarlet fever, typhoid fever, tuberculosis, and venereal diseases), had a drastic impact on the islanders, with the population falling from around 35,000 at the time of first European contact to between 8,000 and 9,000 in the early nineteenth century and under 6,000 by the time of the 1854 French census (Oliver, 1974).

Whalers and merchants had a profound impact on the islanders and their culture. So too did missionaries, initially Protestants from the London Missionary Society, whose aim was conversion to Christianity and, with it, the imposition of their concept of what constituted respectable civilization. The conversion to Christianity of Pōmare II in 1812, along with missionary support for his efforts to retain and further his control, were significant factors in his overall success. By the middle of the second decade of the nineteenth century, Pōmare II, by virtue of a marriage alliance and victory in battle, had become *Ari'i Rahi*, king of Tahiti, uniting Tahiti under the control of a single family. By the end of the decade, the gospels had been translated into Tahitian (*Reo Mā'ohi*) and were being taught in religious schools, Pape'ete had been established as the island capital, and a legal code had been introduced (the Pōmare Legal Code) according to which nudity, dance, chants, flower costumes, and tattoos were banned. By the 1920s, the entire population espoused Protestantism (Mayer, 2016).

When Pōmare II died, his son (Pōmare III) was only eighteen months old. This provided local chiefs with an opportunity to win back some of their powers. It also provided the missionaries with an opportunity to move the monarchy closer in type to that of the English constitutional monarchy and to create a Legislative Assembly. After Pōmare III's death at six years of age in 1827, his thirteen-year-old half-sister 'Aimata took the title of Pōmare IV but had difficulty retaining power.

A struggle for influence between English Protestants and French Catholics then began in earnest. In 1843, Pritchard, the Queen's Protestant advisor, persuaded her to display the Tahitian flag rather than that of the French Protectorate. As a result, during the queen's absence, Admiral Dupetit-Thouars persuaded chiefs who were hostile to the Pōmare family to sign a petition requesting French protection. Pritchard was thrown into prison, and later sent back to Britain, and the queen was exiled to the Leeward Islands before being forced to ratify the agreement. This left her in nominal charge of internal affairs but gave France control over foreign relations, defence, and internal order.

In March 1844, a Franco-Tahitian war began. It ended in December 1846 in favor of the French. In 1847, the queen returned from exile and agreed to sign a new covenant which further reduced her powers. The French were now in control of the Tahitian kingdom. In 1863, they replaced the British Protestant Missions with the *Société des missions évangéliques de Paris*

(Society of Evangelical Missions of Paris). While these events were taking place, approximately 1,000 Chinese arrived in Tahiti to work on a cotton plantation, many remaining after the plantation went out of production in 1873.

In 1877, Queen Pōmare died. Her son, Pōmare V, was persuaded to abdicate by the French governor and a number of Tahitian chiefs. On 29 June 1880, he ceded Tahiti to France along with the islands that were its dependencies. Tahiti thus became a special French colony and in 1890 Pape'ete became a *commune* (administrative division) of the Republic of France. From this point on, immigration increased dramatically, with 2,000 of the 12,000 people living in Pape'ete in 1907 being of French metropolitan extraction (Newbury, 1980, pp. 271–272).

In 1903, the French Establishments in Oceania (*Établissements Français d'Océanie*) were created. Tahiti was from then on treated as part of a group of islands that came within the control of the French Republic. In 1946, Tahiti and the whole of French Polynesia were re-designated as an overseas territory (*Territoire d'outre-mer*)[4] and the residents of the islands were given French citizenship. In 1957, the area was renamed French Polynesia (*Polynésie Français*) and in 1958, a constitutional referendum was held to determine whether ties with France would be maintained. Fearing the loss of French financial support, many Polynesians voted for the maintenance of French involvement: the final vote was 64.4 percent in favor of maintaining ties with France. In 2003, French Polynesia's status was changed to that of an overseas collectivity (*collectivité d'outre-mer*),[5] and in 2004 it was declared an overseas country (*pays d'outre-mer*) of the French Republic.[6]

CULTURE

Prior to the arrival of Europeans, Tahiti was divided into territories, each dominated by a single clan led by a chief (*ari'i rahi*) and made up of nobles (*ari'i*) and under-chiefs (*'īato'ai*). Decisions, especially in time of war, were made by groups of nobles and under-chiefs. At the core of each chiefdom was a stone temple (*marae*) which, according to Salmond (2010, pp. 24, 26, 34, 38, 53, 67, 96, 149, 266, 273–274), were "portals between *Po*, the world of the gods and darkness, and the *Ao*, the everyday world of people and light." In most cases, women were not permitted to attend marae ceremonies. Tahitians recognized a series of gods, including one supreme deity (*Ta'aroa*). Thus, for example, *Tāne* was the god of agriculture, *Tū* the artisan god, *'Oro* the god of war (Craig, 1989). Gods and goddesses were viewed as having given birth to the islands which needed to be cherished and protected, with the gods and goddesses requiring propitiation in order for society to operate smoothly.

There were two classes of priest, each of which was involved in sorcery: those who conducted formal rituals, and those who mediated the voices of the gods and provided oracular advice. Illnesses, which were often thought of as the result of sorcery, godly anger or contact with something or someone sacred, were often treated at marae and that treatment could include human sacrifice. Also central to traditional practices was tattooing, with tattoos recording family links, rites of passage and memorable events.

Much labor was spent on terracing and irrigation of the land in preparation for the growth of taro. The fields were controlled by household groups acting through the head of the household. Coconut and breadfruit trees could, however, be owned by individuals as well as by household groups.

Many elements of traditional cultural practices, such as dancing, music, tattooing, and belief in multiple gods and ancestral spirits, almost disappeared under the influence of missionaries. However, with the country's growing independence has come a cultural resurgence, including growing interest in linguistic revival and maintenance. Nevertheless, Christianity has largely supplanted traditional religious practices and the survival of other traditional cultural practices is far from assured. Even so, as in other parts of Polynesia, reciprocity, generosity and hospitality are still considered to be central values.

LANGUAGE

A majority of the residents of the islands speak both French and Tahitian, with some older Chinese speaking the Haka dialect of Chinese. Tahitian appears to be gradually replacing the other Polynesian languages of the region as these languages themselves become more homogeneous.[7] French is, however, the only official language of French Polynesia according to Article 54 of the Constitution, as amended by Constitutional Act 92-554 of 25 June 1992 which reads: *La langue de la République est le français* (The language of the Republic is French). According to an organic law of 12 April 1996, however, Tahitian and other Polynesian languages can be used in the public sphere. Even so, although use of Tahitian and other Polynesian languages is a long established practice in the Assembly of French Polynesia, in 2010 a petition relating to the right to use Polynesian languages in the Assembly was rejected by the European Court of Human Rights (Moyrand & Angelo, 2010).

According to a 2017 census, over 95 percent of those 15 years old and over reported that they could speak, read, and write French and over 86 percent that they had some knowledge of at least one Polynesian language. Also, roughly three quarters reported that they spoke mainly French at home, with just under one quarter reporting that they spoke mainly Tahitian at home. Other languages reportedly spoken at home were: Marquesian (2.6 percent), the Mangareva language (0.2 percent), one of the Austral languages (1.2 percent), Tuamotuan (1.0 percent), a Chinese dialect (0.4 percent), and some other language (0.4 percent). As Temaru, several times elected President of French Polynesia, has noted: "When we started to go to school, we were strictly forbidden to speak our own language" (Green Left Weekly, 1995). As indicated as long ago as 1970 by Robert Levy (1970), Tahitian is being used as a *lingua franca* by Polynesians throughout French Polynesia, with the other indigenous languages being "Tahitanized" and gradually replaced. In addition, among some of the more highly educated Tahitians, bilingualism (French/Tahitian) is being replaced by French monolingualism.

From 1880 until 1981, all levels of schooling were conducted in French. However, a cultural renaissance centered in Tahiti which began in the 1960s finally led to official recognition of the Tahitian language and its reintroduction into the education system in 1982. From 1984, 2 hours and 40 minutes of indigenous language learning (Tahitian or another Polynesian language) each week in elementary and primary schools was finally sanctioned. The official recognition of the Tahitian language also led to its coming under the protection of the French Academy and this, in turn, led to a standardization of the language which has had an inhibiting effect on those, particularly the young, who have become concerned that their Tahitian is somehow sub-standard. Nevertheless, Tahitian is still widely spoken and Charpentier and François (2015) maintain that it has always been the language of protest and the assertion of identity.

English is taught as a third language in most schools, including all of those run by the Chinese community, and it is a prerequisite for some types of employment in the hotel industry (those involving relations with guests). In addition, many young Tahitians are eager to learn English in order to feel themselves to be part of what they see as a desirable American-dominated youth culture (Frommer's French Polynesia Travel Guide, n.d.)

NUCLEAR TESTING

France had been conducting its nuclear testing program in Algeria. In 1954, however, Algeria began a struggle for independence, which was achieved in 1962. One year later, in 1963, General de Gaulle established in Tahiti a *Center for Pacific Experimentation* (*Centre d'Expérimentation du Pacifique*), essentially a nuclear testing center, and one year after that, ignoring protests from the Territorial Assembly, asserted sovereignty over Moruroa[8] and Fangataufa, two atolls that form part of the Tuāmotu Archipelago and are located about one thousand miles east of Tahiti, and announced that these atolls were to become nuclear test sites (Aldrich & Connell, 1998, p. 185). In addition, a lesser known nuclear test site was established at Mangareva and Totegegie in the Gambier Archipelago. Tahitians were, however, told that the testing there would involve only non-nuclear rockets (Barrillot, 2002, p. 113). From this point on, land was gradually stripped from Tahitians, with land prices multiplying eightfold between 1971 and 1983 (Tetiarahi, 1987, p. 54).

Despite objections from thirty members of the Polynesian Territorial Assembly,[9] the first nuclear test was conducted on July 2, 1966, when a plutonium fission bomb was exploded in the lagoon at Moruroa. That explosion is said to have sucked all of the water out of the lagoon, covered the atoll in dead fish and molluscs and spread contamination across the Pacific as far as Peru and New Zealand (Stanley, 2004, p. 15; Weyler, 2004, p. 13). In 1974, under intense international pressure, France abandoned atmospheric testing. However, in 1995, President Jacques Chirac announced that testing was to be resumed. This time, the testing would be underground. There was an immediate negative worldwide response, with as much as two thirds of French people being opposed (Lewis, 2005). In French Polynesia itself, protests, led by Oscar Temaru, then Mayor of Fa'a'ā and leader of the pro-independence party (*Tāvini Huira'atira*), took place on a massive scale. The drilling into volcanic rock beneath the atolls that accompanied the underground testing represented a serious risk of future escape of radioactive materials.[10] The final test took place in January 1996, just a few months before the United Nations General Assembly adopted the *Comprehensive Nuclear-Test-Ban Treaty* (1994) banning all nuclear test explosions. Between 1966 and 1996, the French Government had conducted almost two hundred nuclear bomb tests above and below the atolls of Moruroa (*Hiti-Tautau-Mai*) and Fangataufa. French Polynesia was, however, no longer of the same value to metropolitan France. Thus, in 1996, fearing a total withdrawal of French financial support, President Gaston Flosse entered into an agreement whereby metropolitan France would continue to provide a subsidy. That subsidy would, however, be reduced from US$180 to US$100 million annually over a ten-year period (Kahn, 2000, p. 99).

Attracted by high salaries and free food and housing, around 3,000 Tahitian men signed on to work at nuclear test sites in French Polynesia. The impact on them, and on the whole of French Polynesia and beyond, has been catastrophic. Thus, for example, by 2010, 30 percent of those who worked at Moruroa had become ill with cancer (Ista, 2002, p. 73). Tureia, an atoll about 75 miles north of Moruroa, buried one third of its adult population in the five years between 1977 and 2002, all of them victims of cancer (p. 34). Tahiti was exposed to 500 times the maximum accepted levels of radiation, and elevated levels of thyroid cancers and leukemia have been experienced throughout Polynesia. Islands and atolls have been effectively destroyed and wild life throughout the region has suffered profoundly (Institute for Energy and Environmental Research, 1991 (chapter 9)). It was not, however, until 2010 that France engaged in a limited process of compensation. Even then, although it offered millions of euros in compensation for military and other personnel who had been present at the nuclear sites, a clause indicating that there was negligible risk so far as the rest of the population was concerned made it almost impossible for others to apply successfully (Samuel, 2019).[11] In fact, fewer than twenty people of the many thousands affected have received compensation to date (December 2020) even though President Edouard Fritch told the Assembly in 2018 that he and fellow politicians had lied about the tests for thirty years (Zweifel, 2019) and France, in 2019, finally officially acknowledged that the health of local people could have been affected by the tests (Samuel, 2019).

Even before the nuclear testing began, major change took place in Tahiti. Between 1962 and 1988, there was an almost three-fold increase in the population. With that increase came an economic boom. Many Polynesians moved to the city, abandoning their traditional way of life and their reliance on fishing and the production for export of copra, vanilla, and coffee. Wages rose, house prices and rents soared, and corruption became rampant as social inequalities increased. Then, following the cessation of nuclear testing, there was a massive economic slump (Dropsy & Montet, 2018).

POVERTY AND ALIENATION

Prior to the arrival of Europeans, islanders relied on a subsistence economy, with communities terracing mountains for agricultural production and building stone walls to contain river banks as well as creating coral systems for breeding and retaining fish. Following the arrival of Europeans, there was a move to the shorelines where salt, pork, fruit, and dried fish could be traded with ships' crews. Following European settlement in the islands, there was a further move away from the traditional subsistence economy. Copra, coffee, cotton, vanilla, and oranges as well as black pearls and sandalwood began to be exported. With the exception of vanilla and black pearls, these exports suffered from economic downturns, leaving the islands heavily dependent on the activities surrounding nuclear testing. Following the cessation of nuclear testing, the focus moved to tourism which had become increasingly popular since the opening of an international airport at Fa'a'ā. In 1959, there had been fewer than 1,500 tourists to Tahiti; by 1960, that number had risen to more than 4,000 and to close to 9,000 by 1961 (Covit, 1968, p. 113). Tourism continues to be the main source of foreign exchange. However, it suffered significantly following the 2008 global economic crisis and remains in decline. The severity of that decline is evidenced by the very large number of empty and deteriorating hotels and hotel complexes. As Bachimon (2012, p. 3) notes, tourist wastelands are permanent aspects of the French Polynesian landscape. In 2012, there were twelve abandoned hotel complexes in Tahiti alone, with a further twenty in other parts of French Polynesia (Bachimon, 2012, p. 3). As Kahn (2011, p. 79) observes:

[A]s tourists were arriving in increasing numbers in search of Gaugin's paradise, Tahiti was becoming radically transformed, diverging further from the imagined Tahiti that had caused them to visit. Mass migration of people from the outer islands to Pape'ete resulted in previously unknown phenomena, such as squatter settlements, unemployment, and poverty. (Kahn, 2011, p. 79)

Subsidies from France are now critical to the economic survival of the islands. Though keen to reduce these subsidies, France appears to be willing to maintain at least some level of subsidy so long as the islands remain an important part of its Pacific strategy. Nevertheless, there is extreme poverty in a country in which the cost of living is very high, with the gap between rich and poor now equaling that of Latin American countries. The top 20 percent of households now receive half the total income; the poorest 30 percent now receive only 6 percent (Cornet, 2016). Income tax, first introduced in 1993, is not sufficient to support social welfare services in any way equivalent to those available in metropolitan France. The poor, therefore, rely heavily on social and humanitarian agencies which have set up children's villages for orphaned and abandoned children and shelters for the homeless. The resentment which was so evident in riots following the resumption of nuclear testing in 1995–1996, remains in evidence as French Polynesia struggles with external perceptions of the islands as some sort of Polynesian paradise versus the reality of sewage and pesticide contamination (caused by soil erosion) and the effects of irradiation (Danielson, 1993; Kahn, 2000).

FIGHTING BACK

Beginning with guerrilla warfare led by King Pōmare between 1844 and 1847 (Newbury, 1973), there has been ongoing resistance to French involvement in Tahiti and the other islands of *Te Ao Mā'ohi*. That resistance is often particularly associated with Pouvāna'a Tetuaapua 'Ō'opa who, returning in 1946 from fighting with the Free French forces, found that government jobs in Tahiti continued to be largely unavailable to Polynesians. In 1964, he led a demonstration aimed at preventing French officials from disembarking from French vessels at the dockside. He was arrested and spent several months in jail before being acquitted. In 1949 and again in 1952, he was elected to the French National Assembly and in 1953 his party, the *Rassemblement démocratique des populations tahitiennes*/Democratic rally of the Tahitian people (RDPT) won eighteen out of twenty-five seats in the Territorial Assembly. From that point on, the RDPT, whose ultimate aim was independence, came under attack from those who sought to retain France's influence.

When 'Ō'opa indicated that the RDPT was in favor of independence, President de Gaulle announced that all French aid and support would be cut off immediately should any of France's overseas possessions vote for independence (Angus, 1995). Those against succession (largely French settlers, the Catholic Church hierarchy, civil servants, and military personnel) launched a political campaign that led to a split in the RDPT. Following the 1958 referendum, there was civil unrest in Tahiti. De Gaulle sacked 'Ō'opa and his cabinet and, without any substantive evidence, claimed that he was planning to burn down Pape'ete. 'Ō'opa and twenty-two supporters were arrested and 'Ō'opa was jailed. After a year in solitary confinement, he was sentenced to eight year's jail and fifteen years' exile. In 1963, the RDPT was outlawed after it opposed plans for a nuclear testing program. 'Ō'opa was pardoned in 1968 and was elected to the French Senate in 1971, serving there until he died in 1977. In 1982, a monument was erected in his memory in front of the Assembly of French Polynesia.

Throughout the 1970s and early 1980s, local politics was dominated by a range of parties calling for greater autonomy. In particular, in 1977, Oscar Temaru formed a pro-independence party called *Front pour la Libération de la Polynésie* (Front for the Liberation of Polynesia (FLP)).[12] A few concessions, all relatively minor, were made and although pro-French parties failed to gain majority support, the demands of the FLP were repeatedly opposed.

Militancy grew and a five party coalition, *Union pour la Démocratie* (Union for Democracy), was formed, winning a victory at the parliamentary elections of 2004 and, following loss of a no-confidence vote, again in 2005. In 2007, 2009, and 2011, Oscar Temaru was elected President of French Polynesia for the third, fourth, and fifth times.

EXPLORING THE LINGUISTIC LANDSCAPE
OF DOWNTOWN PAPE'ETE

Introducing the Site

During my last visit to Tahiti in December 2019, I was based in *Avenue du Prince Hinoi*, just a few hundred meters from the site of makeshift accommodation behind rags and pieces of corrugated iron. My focus was on street names and signs relating to commercial operations in central Pape'ete, the area covered being contained within a rough rectangle running from *Avenue Prince Hinoi* through Boulevard Pomare (orig. Boulevard Pōmare), turning left into *Rue Cook* and left again into *Rue des Poilus Tahitiens* and then on through *Rue Dumont D'Urville* and left again into *Rue des Remparts* and back to *Avenue Prince Hinoi*. This is an area that is widely shown on tourist maps. I also included the nuclear testing memorial site that is located in Paofai (orig. Pā'ōfa'i) Park on the sea walk (off *Boulevard Pōmare*).

Street Names

So far as street names are concerned, I was immediately reminded of the colonial nature of Pape'ete and of the fact that this is a site in which the métropole attempts to reproduce itself (Kahn, 2011, p. 45). All of the street names in the area surveyed, the central city, were in French (although the names of suburbs were, in fact, in Tahitian). Several had names that are directly reminiscent of the names of streets in metropolitan French cities but which seem to have either no connection with French Polynesia or, at best, a very tenuous one. These include *Rue Jeanne d'Arc* (heroine of the Hundred Year's War and one of only two women commemorated in the street names observed), *Rue du Maréchal Foch* (the General who served as Supreme Allied Commander of the Western Front in World War I), and *Avenue Clémenceau* (Prime Minister of France from 1906 to 1909 and 1917 to 1920). Note that in the sign in Figure 5.1 the heading "TITIAIVAI" (orig. 'TITI'AIVAI') which is the name of a suburb of Pape'ete, is a Tahitian word. The irony is, however, that it is the name that was given to a type of fish and a type of tidal plant, both of which were common before the land reclamation that was involved in the establishment of the city.

Occupying a central city position and starting from the cathedral is the *Rue du General de Gaulle,* which commemorates the man who was not only leader of the Free French movement during World War II but was also President of France from 1958 until 1969. It was he who was responsible for the sacking of 'Ō'opa and his cabinet and for the jailing of 'Ō'opa. It was also he who declared that France would cease providing aid immediately if there were to be a vote in favor of independence. He was in power when nuclear testing was proposed and also when it began. On a visit to Tahiti in 1966, when a nuclear bomb was about to be exploded, he declared that France appreciated French Polynesia's service in support of peace (by becoming a nuclear testing center) and predicted a great future in which the country would become an essential center of the great communications network of the Pacific.

Figure 5.1   Street Name in Central Pape'ete. *Source:* Photo Credit Diane Johnson.

Many of the street names are associated with World War I and World War II, wars into which French Polynesia was drawn because of its colonization by France. Associated in particular with France's role in World War I are:

Rue des Poilus Tahitiens; Rue du 22 septembre; Rue de La Cannonière Zélée; and Rue de Commandant Destremeau

The *Rue des Poilus Tahitiens* commemorates the almost 1,200 Polynesians who volunteered to defend France during World War I, making up a battalion referred to as the *Bataillon mixte du Pacifique* (Mixed Pacific Batallion) of whom 300 did not return.

The French gunboat Zélée was sunk by the Germans on September 22, 1914 in the port of Pape'ete at the start of World War I. It happened during a German bombardment whose main aim was to secure the over 500 tons of coal stocks that had been stored on the island by the French. Hence the naming of *Rue de La Cannonière Zélée* and *Rue du 22 Septembre*. Perhaps an additional reason for the latter is that the September 22 is a date of particular significance to metropolitan France in that it was on September 22, 1792 that France became a republic.

At the time of the German attack in 1914, Pape'ete had no wireless station and only twenty-five colonial infantry and twenty gendarmes. Against formidable odds, Lieutenant Maxime Destremau, who was the commander of the Zélée, organized the defense of the island, training the few troops available and placing guns from the Zélée on shore to assist in the defense of the city. Although, on orders from France, he eventually sacrificed the Zélée, he nevertheless succeeded in keeping the German battleships at a distance and preventing them from securing the coal stocks. The *Rue de Commandant Destremeau* is named in his honor.

Associated with World War II are:

Rue Edouard Ahnne and *Rue Lagarde*

The *Rue Edouard Ahnne* commemorates Edouard Ahnne who arrived in Tahiti in 1892 as a missionary for the *Société des missions évangéliques de Paris* (Paris Society of Evangelical Missions). He subsequently became a school principal, Curator of the Pape'ete Museum, and President of the Society for Oceanic Studies. When France collapsed in 1940, and following an appeal by General de Gaulle, he persuaded Governor Jean Chastenet de Géry to consult the population on rallying Tahiti in support of de Gaulle's Free French forces and many subsequently joined the Pacific Batallion. He was made a *Compagnon de la Libèration* (Companion of the Liberation) and *Chevalier de la Légion d'honneur* (Knight of the Legion of Honour).

Rue Lagarde is named after Georges Auguste Felix LaGarde who was a French-Tahitian interpreter and Justice of the Peace in The Marquesas Islands and the Leeward Islands from 1903 until 1913. He, like Ahnne, lobbied in favor of Free France in French Polynesia and became a member of the provisional government for Free France.

In a number of cases, the street names observed commemorate French exploration of the Pacific and/or those Frenchmen who, including missionaries and government functionaries, played a role in the process of colonization. These include:

Rue Dumont D'Urville; *Rue de L'Arthémise*; *Rue Nansouty*; *Rue du Petit Thouars*; *Rue Vénus*; *Avenue Bruat*; and *Rue Mgr T. Jauseen*; *Rue Colette*; *Rue François Cardella* and *Rue de Anne-Marue Jovouhey*

Rue Dumont D'Urville is named after Jules Sébastien César Dumont d'Urville who was born in 1790 in Normandy. He commanded voyages of exploration to the South Pacific from 1826 until 1829 and again from 1837 until 1840. In 1822, he boarded the ship *La Coquille*, captained by Louis Duperrey, which was bound for the Pacific, his main role being that of botanist, entomologist and cartographer. *La Coquille* brought back to France specimens of more than 3,000 species of plants, 400 of which were previously unknown. In 1826, as captain of the *Astrolabe* (the renamed *Coquille*), he set out toward the Pacific, aiming to circumnavigate the world. During that journey, he prepared the first relief maps of the Loyalty Islands. An excellent linguist and accomplished cultural observer as well as cartographer, he was responsible for identifying a range of different Pacific island groups and peoples. On return to France after his final voyage, which began in 1837, he was promoted to rear admiral and awarded the gold medal of the Société de Géographie (Geographical society of Paris). Many places are named after D'Urville. These include the D'Urville Sea (off Antarctica), D'Urville Island, D'Urville Wall, Mount D'Urville and the Dumont d'Urville Station (Antarctic), the Rue Dumont d'Urville, (Paris), the Lycée Dumont D'Urville (Caen), and D'Urville Island (New Zealand).

Rue de L'Arthémise appears to be named after a French frigate which was launched in 1792. Captain La Place was in charge of the frigate in Sydney when he was ordered to make his way to Tahiti to prepare the way for the arrival of Catholic missionaries. When his ship was damaged, Queen Pōmare arranged for Tahitians to assist with its repair.

Rue Nansouty and *Rue Clappier* commemorate French military men who were killed in the Franco-Tahitian war which took place after Queen Pōmare had taken refuge in Ra'iātea in 1844. Following a battle at Maghaena where the French lost 15 men and the Tahitians lost 102, the French attempted to take control of the three neighboring Leeward Islands kingdoms—Ra'iātea, Huahine and Bora Bora—which had traditionally owed allegiance to the Pōmare family. However, it was agreed between France and Britain that these three kingdoms would remain independent. In spite of this, France annexed the Leeward Islands in 1897.

Running off from *Rue du Général de Gaule* is *Rue du Petit Thouars*, commemorating Abel du Petit Thouars who, during a round-the-world voyage on the frigate Vénus (hence *Rue Vénus*) from 1836 to 1839, was sent (in 1838) to seek reparation following the expulsion, on the recommendation of the Queen's Protestant advisor (then acting as British Consul) of two French Catholic priests, Laval and Caret. It was he who persuaded chiefs hostile to the Pōmare family to request protection from France and to sign a treaty of friendship which guaranteed the rights of French subjects, including any future Catholic missionaries to the islands. It was also he who, returning to Tahiti four years later, claimed that the Tahitians had violated the Treaty and prevailed upon Queen Pōmare to agree to ratify the request for protection, write to the King of France apologizing for the mistreatment of the priests, pay reparations and arrange for a salute of the French flag. Queen Pōmare and her family fled aboard the British ship *HMS Basilisk* and went into exile on the neighboring island of Ra'iātea and Pritchard was imprisoned and deported. Although The French government initially disapproved of some of his decisions, believing that they could lead to damaging conflict with Britain,

Thouars was eventually lauded for taking action that led to France's colonization of the region.

Avenue Bruat is named after Armand Joseph Bruat, a French admiral who was made Governor of the Marquesas Islands in 1943 after he had fought off an insurrection formented by the English. He also served as French agent at the court of Queen Pōmare and played a role in persuading her to accept France in a protectorate role. In 1847, he was promoted, becoming a Grand Officer of the French *Légion d'honneur* (Legion of Honor). In 1852, he was given the title of Vice-Admiral.

Rue Mgr T. Jauseen is named after Florentin-Étienne Jaussen who was the first bishop of Tahiti and was responsible for ending slave raids on Easter Island. He ordained the first native priest of Eastern Polynesia, Tiripone Mama Taira Putairi, on December 24, 1874.

Rue Colette is named after Juste François Colette, a Catholic missionary who was responsible for the building of a church on Faa'a in the suburbs of Pape'ete and in 1869 became the first parish priest of Pape'ete. He served as a hospital chaplain and chaplain to the navy, taking part in many expeditions to the outer islands. He also founded a vocational school where children were taught trades such as carpentry and masonry. His practical attitude to the role of missionary was regarded as being too secular and he was sanctioned by the church in 1889 and banned from operating as a priest until the sanction was lifted in 1891, just eight years before he died and was buried in the cemetery of 'Uranie in Pape'ete.

Rue François Cardella commemorates a French pharmacist who became an advisor to King Pōmare V and President of the Colonial Council and the General Council (both of which, before they were disbanded, lobbied for some representation for the people of Tahiti in the face of the overarching power of the governor). He was also Mayor of Pape'ete from 1890 until 1917.

Rue de Anne-Marue Jovouhey is named after the founder of the Sisters of Saint Joseph of Cluny who is known for having been responsible for the freeing of slaves in the French colony of Cayenne. The Congregation of the Sisters of St Joseph of Cluny established three communities in Tahiti and one in the Marquesas.

In the case of *Place Notre Dame*, the street is named after the *Cathédrale* Notre *Dame de L'Immaculée Conception* (Our Lady of the Immaculate Conception*)* in Pape'ete, the cathedral itself being named in accordance with French Catholic tradition and being one of the last examples of early colonial architecture in Tahiti.

In the area surveyed, there were, in addition to the *Rue des Poilus Tahitiens* (see reference above), only four streets which commemorate Tahitian people.

What each of these names has in common is the fact that it commemorates someone who played a role of some kind in ceding Tahitian rule and/or in securing, maintaining or supporting French rule. These are:

Boulevard Pōmare; Avenue de la Reine Pōmare; Avenue Prince Hinoi; Rue du Chef Teri'iero'oitera'i

Boulevard Pomare is named after the reigning family of the Kingdom of Tahiti which lasted from the unification of the island by Pōmare I in 1788 until Pōmare V's cession of the kingdom to France in 1880. In this connection, it is particularly relevant to bear in mind that:

- the French first assisted in the establishment of the Pōmare kingdom and then secured its dissolution;
- the conversion of Pōmare II to Christianity in 1812 was an important factor in the subsequent widespread conversion to Christianity and, along with it, the acceptance of a range of Western cultural norms;
- it was following French collusion with disaffected chiefs that Queen Pōmare (after whom *Avenue de la Reine Pomare (orig. Pōmare)* is named) was forced to agree to their request for French protection;
- it was Queen Pōmare's son, Pōmare V, who ceded Tahiti to France.

Avenue Prince Hinoi is named after the last son of Queen Pōmare, therefore, a member of the Pōmare dynasty, who was adopted by Teri'itua, the female chief of the Hitia'a district. He succeeded Teri'itua, taking her name. However, the name "Joinville" was given to him by the French governor in honor of François, Prince of Joinville, one of the sons of French King Louis Philippe I. The Tahitians translated "Joinville" as "Tuavira," his full name therefore becoming Prince Teri'itua Tuavira Joinville Pōmare. He was, however, widely known as Prince Hinoi. Aged fifteen, with the support of the French governor, he was sent with a group of young Polynesians to France to complete his education. He lived in France from 1862 until 1865, became fluent in French and subsequently acted as an interpreter. He married a woman of English and Tahitian descent.

 Rue du Chef Teriiero_oitera (orig. *Teri'iero'oitera'i*) is named after Teri'iero'o a Teri'iero'oitera'i, a descendant of the customary chiefs of Tahiti. After becoming a postman and then a teacher, he was made chief of the Papeno'o District by the Governor General of French Polynesia. During World War II, he encouraged French Polynesians to join the Free French armed forces and was awarded a *Croix de la Libération* (Liberation cross) by General de Gaulle. He became an officer of the Legion of Honor and a Companion of the Liberation.

Overall, in the area surveyed, there were twenty-five streets. Of these, the names of three, while having significance for metropolitan France, appear to have no particular significance for Tahiti or French Polynesia. Of the remaining twenty-two:

- One commemorates one of the people who must bear primary responsibility for French nuclear testing in the Pacific;
- Six commemorate people or events associated with World Wars I and II, wars into which Pacific islands were drawn largely by virtue of their value to the primary combatants as strategic locations in relation to warfare and/ or as sources of additional fighting power;
- Eleven commemorate French exploration, appropriation and control of Pacific lands, peoples and cultures; and
- Four commemorate members of the Pōmare dynasty, all of whom, either willingly or as a result of coercion and/or manipulation, acted in ways that ultimately supported the cause of France in relation to its colonial ambitions.

The streets whose names feature here are all located at the center of Pape'ete, the capital city of the once remote islands and atolls, located approximately 1,700 km distant from metropolitan France, that are now, taken together, considered to make up a single country under the jurisdiction of the French Republic. These names, written in the French language, present a partial, biased, homogenized, and truncated history that takes little, if any, account of a *ma'ohi* perspective on time, place, language and culture. What is involved is the sanitization and glorification of exploitation, manipulation, conquest, subjugation, deceit and slaughter.

Signs Associated with Central City Commercial Establishments

What was immediately apparent about the names of commercial establishments and the other signs associated with them in the area surveyed was the fact that only approximately 18 percent were in French only, with approximately 5 percent being in English only, and 65 percent in a combination of French and English. In the case of signs in which both French and English featured, English was the more prominent of the two languages in terms of size, position, and script type in most cases. Additionally, where English and French were used in combination, the name of the establishment was generally in English, with words in French providing information or extension of some kind. Translation was found to occur very infrequently (in approximately 2 percent of cases where English and French were found in combination). In spite of the fact that a majority of the residents of Tahiti can speak some Tahitian, with roughly one quarter claiming to speak mainly Tahitian at home, few signs combined French and Tahitian, English and Tahitian, or French, English, and Tahitian (approximately 7 percent in total), with only approximately 2 percent being exclusively in Tahitian. Signs in Japanese only or combining Japanese and another language were extremely rare (approximately 1 percent), as were signs involving language fusion, that is, signs combining two or more languages in a single phrase or sentence (approximately 2 percent).

In connection with the nature of the central city commercial signage observed, it is particularly relevant to bear in mind France's determined attempt to ensure that the French language is maintained as the preeminent language of metropolitan France and its territories. The pressure on colonized peoples to adopt French at the expense of their own languages has been regulatory, judicial, and ideological. Even so, it has proved difficult to maintain in the face of international pressure and has, as a result, been gradually eroded. One of France's responses to the founding of the European Union, and the consequent increased threat from the English language, was to amend its Constitution in such a way

Figure 5.2   Examples of Signs in English in Central Pape'ete. *Source:* Photo Credit Diane Johnson.

Figure 5.3   Examples of Signs in a Combination of French and English in Central Pape'ete. *Source:* Photo Credit Diane Johnson.

Figure 5.4 **Examples of Signs in Tahitian in Central Pape'ete.** *Source:* Photo Credit Diane Johnson.

Figure 5.5 **Example of a Sign in a Combination of French and English Involving Translation.** *Source:* Photo Credit Diane Johnson.

as to make French the official language of the Republic. Another was to fail to ratify the *European Charter for Regional and Minority Languages*. These measures were supplemented by *La loi Toubon*, 1994 (The Toubon Law), the aim of which was to ensure that where a language other than French was used in commercial contexts, that language was accompanied by a French translation of equal prominence. Even in 2008, when France made a minor change to its Constitution which involved the recognition of regional languages, it did not

Figure 5.6   Example of a Sign in a Combination of French, English, and Tahitian in Central Pape'ete. *Source:* Photo Credit Diane Johnson.

accord them official status. Nor was the recognition that was accorded to these languages intended to seriously undermine earlier legal strictures. In view of all of this, it is, perhaps, surprising to find that only approximately 18 percent of the commercial signs in central Pape'ete were found to be in French only, with as many as 65 percent combining English and French and with translation into French being the exception rather than the rule.

During my last visit to Tahiti, I made a point of getting into conversation with as many Tahitian residents as possible, asking, in each case, why they believed so many commercial signs featured English. In most cases (eighteen out of twenty), reference was made to the fact that English is widely used on signage because it is the language spoken by the majority of tourists. However, nine of the eighteen also said that using English was a sign of protest against French rule, arising out of an awareness that French people generally saw English as a threat. Six of the eighteen also noted that both French and English were associated with culture, sophistication and/or wealth and so were appropriate in the case of high-end tourism of the type associated with cruise ships and luxury hotels. The remaining two (of the twenty) simply regarded the use of English as being indicative of the position English has achieved as a result of globalization (see Table 5.1).

Table 5.1 Summary of Responses of Tahitian Participants Regarding Use of Languages in Formulaic Interactions and on Central City Commercial Signage. Author Created

Responses of 20 Tahitian participants	Serves little practical purpose	Makes sense—widely used by tourists	Appropriate (in common with French) for high-end tourism—associated with culture, sophistication, wealth	A sign of protest against French colonization	Assertion of identity/attempt to reclaim place/dignity	Creates/reinforces for tourists a sense of being somewhere exotic
Why is Tahitian not more widely used on commercial signage in the central city?	18					
Why is English so prominent on commercial signage in the central city?		18	6	9		
Why is Tahitian widely used in formulaic interaction, including those with tourists?				7	20	11

Figure 5.7   Example of Language Mixing (French and English in a Single Phrase) on a Sign in Central Pape'ete. *Source:* Photo Credit Diane Johnson.

All twenty of those with whom I had informal conversations were asked about the use of Tahitian on commercial signs in the central city and in conversational contexts. Almost all (18/20) noted that using the Tahitian language on central city signage served little practical purpose because it was not understood by tourists. Even so, almost half (9/20) also noted that they liked to see the language on signs around the city and all twenty believed that the use of Tahitian in day-to-day interactions was an assertion of Polynesian identity and an attempt at reclamation of place and of dignity, with seven adding that it was a way of creating emotional and/or political distance from France as a colonizing power. Eleven also noted that it served a function in relation to tourism, creating/reinforcing the feeling that tourists were somewhere different and/or more exotic, somewhere (as two stressed) other than Europe (see Table 5.1).

None of those with whom I spoke was aware of the regulation regarding translation into French of commercial advertising written in other languages. Overall, the impression gained was that although Tahitians are anxious to assert their Polynesian identity, something that is expressed, in part, in the use of the Tahitian language in formulaic interactions in public spaces, there are practical reasons for their preference for a combination of French and English in public commercial signage in the central city, these reasons relating, in particular, to the perceived needs and attitudes of tourists, At the same time, there is a pervasive sense that use of the French language reinforces French dominance.

Signage Associated with the Nuclear Testing Memorial Site in Pā'ōfa'i Gardens

In November 2018, the French National Assembly voted that the former command complex of the French navy in Pape'ete could be used as the site of a nuclear memorial museum if that museum were to be built within five years. There has, however, been much controversy over this, with some fearing that the presentation would involve sanitization of the nuclear testing process rather than genuine acknowledgment, regret and commemoration (Radio New Zealand, 2018, 2019). Whatever the outcome of the museum proposal, it remains the case that there is already a nuclear testing memorial. That memorial is located in Pā'ōfa'i Gardens on the sea front (just off *Boulevard Pōmare*). It was first unveiled when Oscar Temaru was President of the archipelago—on July 2, 2006, the fortieth anniversary of the first nuclear test on Moruroa. My initial attempts to locate it were unsuccessful. One taxi driver was convinced that it did not exist; another believed that it did exist but was unable to locate it even after consulting several locals. Roaming through the park and still unable to find it, I approached a park warden who very kindly led me to the site which was undergoing renovation. He removed the canvas covering from parts of the monument so that I could see it and take photographs. My first impression was that, in view of the enormity of what is commemorated and the vast expanse of ocean that provide its backdrop, the memorial installation seemed to lack any genuine sense of presence (see Figure 5.8). Nevertheless, reference is made on the monument to all 193 tests and, at the foot of the monument, there are stones representing the islands and atolls most affected. Above all, so far as my primary interest here is concerned, the Tahitian language appears in top position followed by French and then English. Tahitian is, however, the only Polynesian language that features (see Figure 5.9).

CONCLUSION

In relation to struggles over urban space, Jane Jacobs makes the following observation in *Edge of Empire* (p. 4):

> The city is . . . an important component in the spatiality of imperialism. It was in outpost cities that the spatial order of imperial imaginings was rapidly and deftly realized.

Figure 5.8   Nuclear Testing Memorial in Pā'ōfa'i Gardens, Pape'ete. *Source:* Photo Credit Diane Johnson.

The street names of central Pape'ete act as a reminder of the certainty and sense of entitlement of Western colonizers. They celebrate and commemorate conquest and acquisition. They dominate the central city, itself a Western social, cultural and architectural creation, seeking to impose upon it a perspective that is essentially alien and incongruous in this remote archipelago. These names do not, however, make any reference to the events that most define the impact of France on the lives and futures the Polynesian inhabitants of these islands—the nuclear tests. These nuclear tests created a crisis that wholly destabilized an already uncertain relationship between colonizer and colonized, led to a period of severe political turbulence and reinforced the emergent Polynesian cultural renaissance. For those who are aware of these events, as adult Polynesian residents of the city must be, these street names can only be viewed as ironic, particularly in view of the current economic plight of Tahiti and its inhabitants. While the street names proudly announce French presence and French influence, the city itself bears many of the hallmarks of neglect, with abandoned hotels crumbling into ruin, market traders and shopkeepers struggling to attract customers, and shanty settlements barely concealing the poverty and hopelessness of some of the residents of this once proudly held French "possession."

Figure 5.9 One of the Pillars of the Nuclear Testing Memorial in Pā'ōfa'i Gardens, Pape'ete. *Source:* Photo Credit Diane Johnson.

Contrasting with the implicit assertion of French dominance associated with the street names is the almost total disregard for French law as it relates to language planning that is evident in the signs associated with commercial premises. What is apparent here, above all, is the encroachment of English, the language whose international impact has been most feared by those for whom the survival and purity of the French language is a critical aspect of French identity. Although this might at first sight appear to be *wholly* attributable to the tourist-dominated nature of the current Tahitian economy, any such interpretation is called into question by the responses of those Tahitians who took part in the conversations referred to earlier, almost half of whom interpreted the use of English on these signs as a form of protest against French colonization. While the fact that the Tahitian language appeared on only 9 percent of central city commercial signage was generally seen as being practically motivated, its presence was nevertheless appreciated.

Furthermore, the prevalence of the Tahitian language in formulaic interactions with tourists was seen not only as reinforcing their sense of being somewhere exotic but also as an assertion of Polynesian/ Tahitian identity. Overall, the central city commercial signage can be seen as representing a type of resistance to colonial authority, passive in some cases, active in others.

Of the three locations explored, in only one was the Tahitian language prioritized—the nuclear monument in Pā'ōfa'i Gardens. On all of the signage associated with that site, the Tahitian language was followed by French and then English. Sadly, however, no other languages of the archipelago were in evidence and the monument itself appeared to have been largely forgotten. It certainly did not feature in any of the tourist literature that I encountered. And yet that monument commemorates one of the most defining moments in the history of the archipelago, a moment that changed forever the lives of its inhabitants and their relationship with those proud conquerors who set out as members of *les races supérieures* (superior races) to *civiliser* (civilize) *les races inférieures* (the inferior races) and, in the process, created a city at sea, a city whose signage reinforces the sense that it is a space that is wholly out of place.

NOTES

1. Cook had the rank of lieutenant during this first voyage, being promoted to captain later.

2. The aim was to prevent others from gaining a base in the Pacific from which the coast of Peru could be attacked and, in the process, to evangelize.

3. It was believed they would be useful for feeding African slaves.

4. An overseas territory of France is a territorial authority integrated into the French Republic.

5. An overseas collectivity is an administrative division of France with a semi-autonomous status.

6. A French overseas country is simply a renamed overseas collectivity.

7. The languages of French Polynesia are all closely related. They are: 'eo 'enana; 'eo'enata [2 *Marquesan dialects*]; reo vāhitu; reo nāpuka; reo mihiro; reo fangatau [*dialects of the Tūamotu Archipelago*]; reo maupiti; reo tahiti [dialects of the Society Islands]; reo parata [Tuāmotu]; reo tapuhoe [Tuāmotu]; reo maragai [Tuāmotu]; reo rurutu [Austral Islands]; reo mangareva [Gambier Islands]; reo tupua'i [Austral Islands]; reo rimatara [Austral]; reo ra'ivavae [Austral]; and reo rapa [Austral].

8. The French renamed Moruroa (meaning "big lies") as Mururoa (Kahn, 2011, p. 72).

9. A Tahitian Assembly was first established in 1824. However, in its current form, the French Polynesian Assembly (*Assemblée de la Polynésie française; Te âpooraa rahi o te fenua Māòhi*), located in Pape'ete, was established in 1996. It has fifty-seven members who are elected by popular vote for five years.

10. In fact, in 1979, a nuclear device exploded at half the usual depth causing major problems.

11. Eligibility requirements were subsequently relaxed. They were, however, tightened again in 2018 when a clause was introduced into the French finance act defining the minimum level of exposure required for compensation in such a way as to ensure that very few victims would be eligible.

12. Its name was changed in 1983 to *Tāvini Huira'atira* (*People's Servant Party*).

Conclusion

Signs of the Times?

For centuries, the vast Pacific Ocean and its thousands of islands and atolls have had an irresistible attraction for explorers and adventurers from other parts of the world. They have also held an irresistible attraction for rulers and politicians who have been intent on extending their economic bases and spheres of influence. The Pacific was largely colonized at a time of maximum optimism and certainty regarding Western beliefs and practices. Above all, it was a time when confidence in the efficacy of Western development was almost absolute. For Westerners, the possibility that those whose lands and beliefs they trampled on might have lifestyles superior to their own was almost unimaginable, as was the possibility that these people's belief systems were at least of equal value to their own. The ultimate failure of the West to create a secure future for its own people and those they chose to exercise power over could not have been foreseen. Nor could the disastrous consequences of industrialization and globalization for the planet as a whole. The colonizers had a vision of themselves and their activities that was almost entirely positive. What they brought they believed was civilization; what they took was nothing more than that to which they felt entitled. Lands have been stolen. Cultures have been ridiculed. Languages have been silenced. And yet, there is resistance. Meanings and identities are open to contestation, especially at times of crisis. And evidences of that contestation are often to be found in linguistic landscapes.

Each of the studies reported here was preceded by some destabilizing crisis that highlighted the contingency of meanings and identities, a crisis that created an opportunity for the disruption of the *status quo* and the establishment of a new hegemony. This is particularly evident in the case of the Hawaiian study where the linguistic landscape explored was set against the majesty of Maunakea. In stark contrast to the English only "official" signage, generally involving directives (largely prohibitives), was the linguistically diverse signage of the protesters. That signage, reinforced by culturally specific images, positioned the protesters as *US* and those who would violate the mountain and threaten its majesty and species diversity as *OTHER*. The colonizers had become outsiders, excluded culturally and linguistically from an ever-growing community of indigenous peoples and their supporters. Messages of opposition and hope originating from a bleak mountainside in an isolated archipelago were reinforced and amplified as they were beamed around the world, attracting a growing community of environmental protectors determined to resist further depredation and environmental hooliganism.

Although crises create opportunities for resistance, the form that resistance takes may differ widely. The residents of Tirau, in common with residents of agricultural communities around Aotearoa/New Zealand, were faced in the late 1970s and the 1980s with an economic crisis so severe that it threatened their very survival. Suicides in agricultural communities were commonplace. The main reason for this economic downturn was Britain's decision to enter, in 1973, into what was then the European Economic Community (EEC), negotiating with the EEC only a partial and temporary solution to the problems that would inevitably result from the withdrawal of its longstanding preferential trade agreements with its former colony. This situation was exacerbated by a world-wide recession. And yet, although Britain's effective abandonment of its former colony created widespread anger and resentment throughout the country as a whole, many European settlers and their descendants appear to have failed to understand their own role in the pervasive and corrosive ongoing impact of colonialism. It is only with this in mind that it is possible to understand some of the undertones of the recreated landscape of Tirau's commercial district as reviewed in 2016 and 2019. In spite of the fact that the township was established in an area of significant Māori occupation, has a Māori name and a population of whom over a quarter are Māori, and in spite of the important role Māori now play in the country's tourism sector, the linguistic landscape of the township's commercial center was found to be dominated by the English language, reinforced by the almost total absence of Māori images and symbols. This highlights some of the realities of settler colonialism in Aotearoa. The country has been effectively self-governing since 1852, many Māori tribes are becoming increasingly economically powerful following Waitangi Tribunal settlements and there has been an ongoing Māori linguistic and cultural renaissance since the 1970s. None of this, however, appears to have significantly dented the certainties of some later settlers. Toward the end of the twentieth century, the colonial fantasy of New Zealand as an agricultural nation built almost wholly on the backs of sturdy, hard-working European settlers, in which Māori were largely invisible, was in ruins. Even so, the mythic rural idyll that replaces it in Tirau's main drag obliterates Māori as effectively as did the original myth. This is something that was not lost on the Māori interviewees or, it would appear, on whoever chose to fly a Māori independence flag from a house visible from the main road through Tirau.

In the case of Kanaky/New Caledonia, the focus was on the linguistic landscape of the *Jean-Marie Tjibaou* Cultural *Centre* (CCT) and the *Federation of Lay Works* (FOL). The study took place in June 2019. This was just over thirty years after the Matignon Agreements, just over twenty years after the opening of the *Jean-Marie Tjibaou Cultural Centre* (CCT), and just over six months after a referendum in which pro-independence Kanaks were heartened by the unexpected narrowness of the voting margin and, therefore, the prospect of a possible victory at any subsequent independence referendum. Although the reason for the construction of the CCT was, avowedly, the promotion of Kanak linguistic and cultural heritage, the narratives associated with the building itself were calculated from the beginning to contribute to France's attempt to position itself as a continuing force in the Pacific. It was, therefore, not surprising to find that Kanak languages appeared to play a very minor role in the linguistic landscape of the Center, with three international languages, including French, playing a dominant role and reinforcing the overall sense that the building stands at least as much as a testament to French language, style and authority as it does to the languages and cultures of the Kanak peoples.

The desolation of the *Federation of Lay Works* (FOL) building, abandoned and awaiting demolition in the very center of Noumea, could not have been more different from the architectural splendor of the *Jean-Marie Tjibaou* Cultural *Centre,* nor could the messages conveyed by its graffiti-covered surfaces. Although the words that were detectable among the graffiti on the exterior of the *FOL* showed no evidence of the re-emergence of Kanak languages, there was, nevertheless, evidence that the building had been used to display Kanak protest posters. Perhaps of most significance, however, were the words RÊVONS LA FOL, painted in enormous letters and placed at the very summit of the building, words which, in context, can readily be interpreted as a call to action as well as reflection. This suggests that the confident assertion of colonial authority implied in the discourse surrounding the *Jean-Marie Tjibaou* Cultural *Centre* and in the linguistic landscape of the building itself may yet prove to have been misplaced.

The study conducted in Tahiti took place in December 2019, almost half a century after President de Gaulle announced that France appreciated the country's service in support of peace and predicted a great future for the country, and almost a quarter of a century after the riots following France's resumption of nuclear testing in 1995. It was, in addition, just one year after

Edouard Fritch admitted that the government had lied about the effects of nuclear testing and just a few months after France finally acknowledged that the health of local people could have been affected by the tests. The negative impact of the colonial enterprise was evident everywhere—in the squatter settlements, in the crumbling hotels, and in the market and the shops where traders appeared to be struggling to attract business. And yet the French street names in the central city told a different story—a story of colonial certainty and triumph, of victory and success, of France and the French language writ large in the Pacific. Set against that was the signage associated with central city commercial establishments, signage that seemed to belie the version of history implicit in the naming of the streets. Here, the French regulations regarding the use of language on commercial signage appeared to be having little effect. These regulations were being flouted or ignored or, perhaps, the local people simply had little or no knowledge of them. This would suggest, like so many other things in Tahiti, abandonment by metropolitan France, a lack of interest and involvement now that there was little currently to be gained from this outpost which had once been of some use. The French language was no longer wholly dominant in the central city commercial signage. Although the Tahitian language was in evidence on just under 10 percent of signs, its presence on these signs nevertheless played some role in reinforcing the use of the language in many day-to-day interactions, including the characteristic use of formulaic phrases in Tahitian when addressing visitors and tourists. Perhaps more significant than the use of the Tahitian language on some commercial signage is the fact that both English and French appeared together on well over half of the signs, with the English generally featuring in a more prominent position than the French, and with very little of the English signage being translated into French. While there are several possible reasons for this, perhaps all of them playing some part, it is relevant to note that almost half of the Tahitians who took part in the informal research conversations believed that the prevalence of English on these signs represented a form of protest against French colonization, a conscious move to create an emotional distance from France. While the homogenization of the languages of the archipelago is undeniable, so too is the survival to date of the Tahitian language. Overall, the commercial signage surveyed in 2019 suggests that the pervasive influence of the French language may be on the wane.

The International Year of Indigenous Languages (2019) has come and gone and little, if anything, appears to have changed as a result. The linguistic landscapes of colonized lands continue to signal the neglect of Pacific languages and, with it, the neglect and continuing marginalization of those whose lands have been plundered. There are, however, hopeful signs of resistance, not only in the case of protest movements such as that on Maunakea, but also in less overt forms, as in the case of the commercial signage in downtown Pape'ete. The linguistic landscapes encountered in each of the studies reported here tells us something about the current state of the colonial enterprise, something that is particularly significant at this point in the history of the Pacific and, indeed, of the planet. There is deforestation on a massive scale. There are increasingly vigorous bush fires, and the survival of many species is threatened. Islands and atolls that have been home to communities for centuries are disappearing under the sea. We face a human population explosion at the same time as we experience the loss of linguistic and cultural diversity. The Western powers that so enthusiastically invaded the lands of others are now seeking ways of closing their borders against those who require sanctuary at a time of unprecedented migration. Global warming, and all of the problems associated with it, are, in some measure, the result of the determination of Western powers to own and control the world's peoples and resources, to force on others a belief system and way of life that have proved to be prejudicial to the very survival of life on earth. And now, raising issues associated with globalization, and adding to the horrors of those other coronaviruses which have posed a threat to our way of life, we have Covid-19.

Whatever the answers to these problems might be, should there be any, the West does not appear to have them. Surely now it is time to pay careful attention to the views of those who have been the victims of Western ways of thinking and behaving. Observing the ways in which linguistic landscapes reflect the struggles of the indigenous peoples of the Pacific as they re-emerge as a force to be reckoned with is perhaps one of the many starting points in a journey of rediscovery that may help us to overcome the enormous challenges that we currently face.

References

Accord sur la Nouvelle-Calédonie. (1998). https://www.legifrance.gouv.fr/affichTex
te.do?cidTexte=JORFTEXT000000555817&dateTexte=&categorieLien=id

Accords de Matignon. (1988). http://www.unesco.org/culture/fr/indigenous/Dvd/pj/
KANAK/MATIGNON.pdf

Act to Grant a Representative Constitution to the Colony of New Zealand 1852. http:
//nzetc.victoria.ac.nz/tm/scholarly/tei-GovCons-t1-body-d1-d1.html

Adamson, R. (2007). *The defence of French: A language in crisis.* Multilingual
Matters.

Aldrich, R., & Connell, J. (1988). *The last colonies.* Cambridge University Press.

Ammann, R. (1997). *Kanak dance and music.* Agence de Développement de la
Culture (Nouméa, New Caledonia).

Anaya, J. (2011). *Report of the Special Rapporteur on the rights of indigenous
peoples: The situation of Kanak people in New Caledonia, France.* Human Rights
Council, Eighteenth session, Agenda Item 3.

Angus, I. (1995, July 22). Tahiti's independence movement revives. *Green left
Weekly, 195.* https://www.greenleft.org.au/content/tahitis-independence-movemen
t-revives

Arvin, M. (2019, 27 July). *Mauna Kea protests are part of a long fight against
colonialism.* Truthout. https://truthout.org/articles/mauna-kea-protests-are-part-of
-a-long-fight-against-colonialism/

Austin, J. L. (1962). *How to do things with words.* Clarendon Press.

Bachimon, P. (2012). Les friches touristiques en Polynésie française—Révélateur
d'une crise de la destination et forme de résistance au tourisme international
[Tourist brownfields in French Polynesia—Revealing a destination crisis and a
form of resistance to international tourism]. *Tourism Review, 1.* https://journals.ope
nedition.org/viatourism/1318

Backhaus, P. (2007). *Linguistic landscapes: A comparative study of urban
multilingualism in Tokyo.* Multilingual Matters.

Backhaus, P. (2015). Attention please! A linguistic soundscape/landscape analysis of ELF information provision in public transport in Tokyo. In K. Murata (Ed.), *Exploring ELF in Japanese academic and business contexts: Conceptualization, research and pedagogic implications* (pp. 194–209). Routledge.

Balfour Declaration 1926. https://www.foundingdocs.gov.au/resources/transcripts/c th11_doc_1926.pdf

Barni, M., & Bagna, C. (2010). Linguistic landscape and language vitality. In E. Shohamy, E. Ben Rafael, & M. Barni (Eds.), *Linguistic landscape in the city* (pp. 3–38). Multilingual Matters.

Barni, M., & Bagna, C. (2016). 1 March—'A day without immigrants': The urban linguistic landscape and the immigrants' protest. In R. Blackwood, E. Lanza, & H. Woldemariam (Eds.), *Negotiating and contesting identities in linguistic landscapes* (pp. 55–70). Bloomsbury.

Barni, M., & Vedovelli, M. (2013). Linguistic landscapes and language policies. In C. Hélot, M. Barni, R. Janssens, & C. Bagna (Eds.), *Linguistic landscapes, multilingualism and social change* (pp. 27–38). Peter Lang.

Barrillot, B. (2002). *L'heritage de la bombe: Sahara, Polynésie 1960–2002.* Centre de Documentation et de Recherche sur la Paix et les Conflits.

Bas-Lauriol Law 1975 (La loi n°75-1349 du 31 décembre 1975 relative à l'emploi de la langue française). https://www.legifrance.gouv.fr/affichTexte.do?cidTexte= JORFTEXT000000521788&idArticle=LEGIARTI000006421237&dateTexte =vig

Beckwith, M. W. (2016). The *Hawaiian romance of Laieikawa.* Wentworth Press.

Belich, J. (1986). *The New Zealand wars.* Penguin Books.

Belich, J. (1996). *Making peoples: A history of New Zealanders from Polynesian settlement to the end of the nineteenth century.* University of Hawaii Press.

Bensa, A. (2000). *Ethnologie et architecture: Le Centre culturel Tjibaou, Nouméa, Nouvelle-Calédonie, une réalisation de Renzo Piano.* Adam Biro.

Bhatia, T. K. (2000). *Advertising in rural India: Language, marketing, communication and consumerism.* Institute for the Study of Languages and Cultures of Asia and Africa, Tokyo University.

Biddle, J. (2003). Country, skin, canvas: The intercorporeal art of Kathleen Petyarre. *Australian and New Zealand Journal of Art, 4*(1), pp. 61–76.

Biggs, B. (1968), The Maori language past and present. In F. Schwimmer (Ed.), *The Maori people in the nineteen-sixties: A symposium* (pp. 65–84). Hurst & Co.

Billotte Laws 1969 (Lois de Bilotte). https://juridoc.gouv.nc/juridoc/jdwebe.nsf/jo ncentry?openpage&ap=1969&page=65

Blackwood, R. J., & Tufi, S. (2015). *The linguistic landscape of the mediterranean.* Palgrave Macmillan.

Bouge, L.-G. (1953). *Pomare, King of Tahiti.* Tahiti: Société des Océanistes.

Brooking, T. (1998). *Milestones: Turning points in New Zealand history.* Mills Publications.

Brown, P. (2002). Book review—Ethnologie et architecture: Le Centre culturel Tjibaou: Une réalisation de Renzo Piano. *Contemporary Pacific, 14*(1), 281–284.

Buchanan, P. (2014). Country risk assessment: New Caledonia. Thirty-sixth-parallel geopolitical and strategic assessments. https://36th-parallel.com/2014/10/22/cou ntry-risk-assessment-new-caledonia/

Chappell, D. (2013). *The Kanak awakening: The rise of nationalism in New Caledonia.* Pacific Islands Monograph Series, *27.* University of Hawaii Press.

Charpentier, J.-M., & Alexandre, F. (2015). *Linguistic atlas of French Polynesia/ Atlas linguistique de la Polynésie française.* De Gruyter Mouton.

Christiansen, I. (2001). Ko te whare whakamana: Māori language revitalisation. Unpublished doctoral dissertation. Massey University, New Zealand.

Constitution Act 1986. http://www.legislation.govt.nz/act/public/1986/0114/latest/D LM94204.html

Constitution of the State of Hawai'i of 1978, Section 5–6.5. http://www.capitol.h awaii.gov/hrscurrent/vol01_ch0001-0042f/hrs0005/hrs_0005-0006_0005.htm

Constitutional Act 92-554 (France), 1992, June 5.

Cornet, R. (2016, December 4). Poverty in French Polynesia. *Borgen Magazine.* https ://www.borgenmagazine.com/poverty-french-polynesia/

Corrugated Country (2010, May 4). Kiwi Crazy: Musings on time misspent at the bottom of the world. https://jocuteca.wordpress.com/tag/corrugated-iron/

Council of Europe (1992, November 4). *European charter for regional or minority languages.* https://www.refworld.org/docid/3de78bc34.html (accessed 24 July 2019).

Coupland, N. (2010). Welsh linguistic landscapes 'from above' and 'from below'. In A. Jaworski & C. Thurlow (Eds.), *Semiotic landscapes: Language, image, space* (pp. 77–101). Continuum.

Covit, B. (1968). *Official directory and guide book: Tahiti, Pape'ete.* l'imprimerie du Gouvernement.

Craig, R. D. (1989). *Dictionary of polynesian mythology.* Greenwood Press.

Cresswell, T., & Martin, C. (2012). On turbulence: Entanglement of disorder and order on a Devon beach. *Tijdkrift vor Economische en Sociale Geografie, 103*(5), 516–529.

Curtin, M. L. (2009). Languages on display: Indexical signs, identities and the linguistic landscape of Taipei. In E. Shohamy & D. Gorter (Eds.), *Linguistic landscape: Expanding the scenery.* Routledge.

Danielson, M. T. (1993). Problems in paradise: The case of Tahiti. *Instraw News, 19,* 47–52.

Davis, C. (2018, January 24). *State says it will provide Hawaiian interpreters in courts to those who request them.* Hawai'i News Now. https://www.hawaiine wsnow.com/story/37344278/state-says-it-will-provide-hawaiian-interpreters-in -courts-to-those-who-request-them/

Dayton, K. (2019, December 20). *Thirty meter telescope protesters told to clear road by Dec. 20.* Star Advertiser. https://www.sThirty Meter Telescope protesters told to clear road by Dec. 26.

de Zayas, A. M. (2018, February 25). *Memorandum to Honourable Gary W. B. Chang, Honourable Jeannette H. Castagnetti abd Members of the Judiciary for the State of Hawaii.* Office of the High Commissioner, United Nations Human Rights. https://hawaiiankingdom.org/pdf/Dr_deZayas_Memo_2_25_2018.pdf

Delaney, J. (2010). *Strait through: Magellan to cook & the pacific*. Princeton University Library.

Dere, L. A. (2012). Urban dictionary: *Da dose*. https://www.urbandictionary.com/def ine.php?term=da%20dose

Dropsy, V., & Montet, C. (2018). Economic growth and productivity in French Polynesia: A long-term analysis. *Economie et Statistique/Economics and Statistics, 499*, 5–27.

Duncan, J. S. (1990). *The city as text: The politics of landscape interpretation in the Kandyan kingdom*. Cambridge University Press.

Education Ordinance. (1847). https://teara.govt.nz/en/zoomify/34874/education-o rdinance-1847

Ethnologue (Pacific). (n.d.). https://www.ethnologue.com/region/pacific

Faberon, J.-Y., & Postic, J-R. (2004). *L'accord de Nouméa: La loi organique et d'autres documents juridiques et politiquers de la Nouvelle-Calédonie*. Île de Lumières.

Fairclough, N. (1995). *Critical discourse analysis: The critical study of language*. Longman.

Ferry. (1884, March 28). *On French colonial expansion, trans*. https://www.thelatin library.com/imperialism/readings/ferry.html

Figueiredo, E., & Rashi, A. (2011). 'Un' immense campagna avvolta dal verde': Reinventing rural landscapes in Italy through tourism promotional images. *European Countryside, 3*(1), 1–20. http://www.degruyter.com/view/j/euco.2011.3 .issue-1/v10091-011-0001-4/v10091-011-0001-4.xml?format=INT

Finnerty, R. (2019, August 21). *Police boost traffic enforcement near Hawaii telescope protest*. Associated Press (Hawai'i Public Radio). https://www.hawaiipu blicradio.org/post/police-boost-traffic-enforcement-near-hawaii-telescope-protest #stream/0

Frommer's French Polynesia Travel Guide: Language in French Polynesia. (n.d.). https://www.frommers.com/destinations/french-polynesia/in-depth/language

Green, R. (1966). Linguistic subgrouping within Polynesia: The implications for prehistoric settlement. *The Journal of the Polynesian Society, 75*(1), 6–38.

Grimes, J. E. (1995). Language endangerment in the Pacific. *Oceanic Linguistics, 43*(1), 1–12.

Hall, S., & Jefferson, T. (Eds.). (1976). *Resistance through rituals: Youth subcultures in post-war Britain*. Hutchinson.

Hanauer, D. (2013). Transitory linguistic landscapes as political discourses: Signage at three political demonstrations in Pittsburgh, USA. In C. Hélot, M. Barni, R. Janssens, & C. Bagna (Eds.), *Linguistic landscapes, multilingualism and social change* (pp. 139–154). Peter Lang.

Hanauer, D. I. (2015). Occupy Baltimore: A linguistic landscape analysis of participatory social contestation in an American city. In R. Rubdy & S. Ben Said (Eds.), *Conflict, exclusion and dissent in the linguistic landscape* (pp. 207–222). Palgrave Macmillan.

Hawaii Admission Act. (1959). An act to provide for the admission of the state of Hawaii into the union. http://www.hawaii-nation.org/admission.html

Hawai'i News Now (2019, December 26). *In major deal, TMT protesters agree to temporarily clear Mauna Kea access road.* https://www.hawaiinewsnow.com/2019/12/26/tmt-protesters-move-kupuna-tent-thats-blocking-road-mauna-kea-summit/

Hawaiian Homes Commission Act. (1920, amended 1921). https://www.capitol.hawaii.gov/hrscurrent/vol01_ch0001-0042f/06-Hhca/HHCA_.htm

Hedley, R. (2004). Prototype theory and the concept of *taonga*: Implications for Treaty-related issues such as display and conservation of taonga Māori. *He Puna Kōrero/Journal of Maori and Pacific Development, 5*(1), 49–68.

Herman, D. (2015, April 23). *The heart of Hawaiian Peoples' arguments against the telescope on Mauna kia.* Smithsonian.com. https://www.smithsonianmag.com/smithsonian-institution/heart-hawaiian-people-arguments-arguments-against-telescope-mauna-kea-180955057/#pVYhdC6r50E8gzKO.99

Hiraishi, K. (2018, January 24). *Maui telescope protester battles over Hawaiian language use in court.* Hawai'i Public Radio. https://www.hawaiipublicradio.org/post/maui-telescope-protester-battles-over-hawaiian-language-use-court#stream/0

House of Representatives, State of Hawai'i. (2017, January 24). *Summary description.* https://www.capitol.hawaii.gov/session2018/bills/HB1264_.pdf

Howes, D. (2018, April 10). The skinscape: Reflections on the dermalogical turn. *Body Society, 24*(1–2), 225–239.

Hughes, G. (1992). Tourism and the geographical imagination. *Leisure Studies, 11*(1), 31–42.

Immerwahr, D. (2019). *How to hide an empire: A history of the Greater United States.* Farrar, Straus & Giroux.

Inglis, F. (1977). Nation and community: A landscape and its morality. *Sociological Review, 25*, 489–514.

Institut de la statistique et des études économiques Nouvelle-Calédonie: Tourisme bilan 2014. https://translate.google.com/translate?hl=en&sl=fr&u=http://www.isee.nc/&prev=search

Institute for Energy and Environmental Research. (1991). *Radioactive heaven and earth: The health and environmental effects of nuclear weapons testing.* Apex Press & Zed Books. https://ieer.org/wp/wp-content/uploads/1991/06/RadioactiveHeavenEarth1991.pdf

Ista, D. (2002). Que cesse le silence et les secrets qui ensevelissent nos morts. In M.-C. Beaudeau (Ed.), *Les essais nucléaires et la santé* (pp. 34–35). Centre du Cocumntation et de Recherche sur la Paix et les Conflits.

Jackson, P. (Ed.). (1987). *Race and racism: Essays in social geography.* Allen and Urwin.

Jacobs, J. (1996). *Edge of empire: Postcolonialism and the city.* Routledge.

Jaworski, A., & Thurlow, C. (2010). Introducing semiotic landscapes. In A. Jaworski & C. Thurlow. (Eds.), *Semiotic landscapes: Language, image, space* (pp. 1–40). Continuum.

Johnson, D. (2008). Māori students and issues of hybrid identity: The response of one inner-city state school. *He Puna Kōrero/Journal of Māori and Pacific Development, 9*(2), 67–78.

Johnson, D. (2017). Linguistic landscaping and the assertion of twenty-first century Maori identity. *Linguistic Landscape, 3*(1), 1–24.

Jolly, M. (2001). On the edge? Deserts, oceans, islands. *The Contemporary Pacific, 13*(2), 417–466.

Jones Act/Philippine Autonomy Act 1916. http://www.chanrobles.com/joneslaw.htm

Jones, R. H. (2005). Sites of engagement as sites of attention: Time, space and culture in electronic discourse. In S. Norris & R. H. Jones (Eds.), *Discourse in action: Introducing mediated discourse analysis* (pp. 141–154). Routledge.

Jones, R. H. (2010a). Creativity and discourse. *World Englishes, 29*(4), 467–480.

Jones, R. H. (2010b). Cyberspace and physical space: Attention structures in computer mediated communication. In A. Jaworski & C. Thurlow (Eds.), *Semiotic landscapes: Text, space and globalization* (pp. 151–167). Continuum.

Jørgensen, M., & Phillips, L. (2002). *Discourse analysis: Theory and method.* SAGE.

Ka'ai-Mahuta, R. (2001). The impact of colonisation on te reo Maori: A critical review of the State education system. In T. M. Ka'ai, J. C. Moorfield, M. P. J. Reilly, & S. Mosley (Eds.), *Ki te whaiao: An introduction to e Māori culture and society* (pp. 201–213). Pearson Education.

Kahn, M. (2000). Tahiti intertwined: Ancestral land, tourist postcard, and nuclear test site. *American Anthropologist, 102*(1), 7–26.

Kahn, M. (2011). *Tahiti beyond the postcard: Power, place and everyday life.* University of Washington Press.

Kasarhérou, E. (1992). The new Caledonian museum. In S. Eoe & P. Swadling (Eds.), *Museums and cultural centres in the Pacific* (pp. 161–168). National Capital District, Papua New Guinea National Museum.

Kelly, M. (1956). *Changes in land tenure in Hawaii, 1778–1850.* Unpublished master's thesis. University of Hawai'i , Honolulu.

Kerr, T. (2011, August 18). *A Pacific view: Views of life and work as an astronomer on the Big Island of Hawai'i.* http://apacificview.blogspot.com/2011/08/astronomy -on-mauna-kea.html

Kirkeby, L. (2020, January 30), *Council saves sheepdog i-SITE.* Waikato Times.

Kowasach, M. (2012). Le développement de l'industrie du nickel et la transformation de la valeur de l'environnement en Nouvelle Calédonie. *Journal of Political Ecology, 19*, 202–220.

Kress, G., & van Leeuwen, T. (1988). Front pages: (The critical) analysis of newspaper layout. In A. S. Bell & P. Garrett (Eds.), *Approaches to media discourse* (pp. 186–219). Blackwell.

Kupau, S. (2004). Judicial enforcement of 'official' indigenous languages: A comparative analysis of the Māori and Hawaiian struggles for cultural language rights 495–536. *University of Hawaii Law Review, 26.*

Kupihea, M. (2001). *Kahuna of light: The world of Hawaiian spirituality.* Inner Traditions.

Laclau, E., & Mouffe, C. (1985). *Hegemony and socialist strategy: Towards a radical democratic politics.* Verso.

Landry, R., & Bourhis, R. Y. (1997). Linguistic landscape and ethnolinguistic vitality: An empirical study. *Journal of Languages and Social Psychology, 16*, 23–49.

Leblic, I. (2003). Chronologie de la Nouvelle-Calédonie. *Journal de la Société des Océanistes, 117*, 299–312.

Levy, R. I. (1970). Teaching of the Tahitian language in the schools of French Polynesia. *Journal de la Société des océanistes, 26*, 79–83.

Lewis, B. (2005). *Blowing up paradise*. First Run Icarrus Films.

Lewis, P. (1979). Axioms for reading the landscape: Some guides to the American scene. In D. W. Meinig (Ed.), *The interpretation of ordinary landscapes* (pp. 11–32). Oxford University Press.

Lewis, R. B. (2014). *The application of critical discourse theory: A criterion-referenced analysis of reports relating to language revitalisation in Australia and New Zealand*. Unpublished doctoral dissertation, University of Waikato, New Zealand.

Loi constitutionnelle de modernisation des institutions de la Ve République. (2008, July 23). https://www.conseil-constitutionnel.fr/les-revisions-constitutionnelles/loi-constitutionnelle-n-2008-724-du-23-juillet-2008

Loi d'orientation pour l'outre-mer. (2000). https://www.senat.fr/leg/tas00-020.html

Loi Toubon 1994. https://www.legifrance.gouv.fr/affichTexte.do?cidTexte=LEGITEXT000005616341

Losche, D. (2003). Cultural forests and their objects in New Caledonia, the Forest on Lifou. Australian and New Zealand Journal of Art, *4*, 77–91.

Macalister, J. (2010). Emerging voices or linguistic silence? Examining a New Zealand linguistic landscape. *Multilingua, 29*, 55–75.

Maclellan, N. (2018, April 30). French colonialism in the Blue Pacific. *Asia & Pacific Policy Studies, Special Issue*. https://www.policyforum.net/french-colonialism-blue-pacific/

Maestre, J.-C., & Miclo, F. (1987). *La Constitution de la République Français* (2nd ed.). Economica.

Main, V. (1998, December 2). New Caledonia takes a gamble on beauty. Press (Christchurch, N).

Malinovsky (de), M. (1979). *Seule la victorie est jolie*. Emom Neptune.

Markus, T. A., & Cameron, D. (2002). *The words between the spaces: Buildings and language*. Routledge.

Marten, H. F., Van Mensel, L., & Gorter, G. (2012). Studying minority languages in the linguistic landscape. In D. Gorter, H. F. Marten, & L. V. Mensel (Eds.), *Minority languages in the linguistic landscape* (pp. 1–18). Palgrave Macmillan.

Mayer, A. (2016). *The history of Tahiti*. Create space independent publishing platform.

McBride, L. R. (2000). *The Kahuna: Versatile masters of old Hawai'i*. Petrograph Press.

Meinig, D. W. (1979). Symbolic landscapes: Some idealizations of American communities. In D. W. Meinig (Ed.), *The interpretation of ordinary landscapes: Geographical essays* (pp. 164–192). Oxford University Press.

Melnick, M. J., & Jackson, S. J. (2002). Globalization American-style and reference idol selection: The Importance of athlete celebrity others among New Zealand youth. *International Review of the Sociology of Sport, 37*(3–4), 429–448.

Message, K. (2006, March). Contested sites of identity and the cult of the new. *reCollections: Journal of the National Museum of Australia, 1*(1), 7–28.

Mills, A. (Ed.). (2005). *Hang on to these words: Johnny David's Delgamuukw evidence.* University of Toronto Press.

Moke, K. (2001). *Kahuna of light: The world of Hawaiian spirituality.* Inner Traditions.

Monroe Doctrine of 1821. https://www.ourdocuments.gov/doc.php?flash=false&doc=23

Morgan Report. (1894). *A report to the US senate and its committee on foreign relations.* https://morganreport.org/mediawiki/media/e/e4/The_Morgan_Report_(3_parts).pdf

Moyrand, A., & Angelo, T. (2010). Can the Polynesian languages be used in the Proceedings of the Assembly of French Polynesia? *New Zealand Association of Comparative Law Yearbook, 16*, 127–134.

Mühlhäusler, P. (2002). *Linguistic ecology: Language change and language imperialism in the Pacific region.* Routledge.

Murphy, B. (2002). Centre Culturel Tjibaou: A museum and arts centre redefining New Caledonia's cultural future. *Humanities Research, 9*(1), 77–90. http://press-files.anu.edu.au/downloads/press/p12791/pdf/8_Murphy.pdf

National Lawyers Guild. (2019, posted 2020, January 13). *NLG calls upon US to immediately comply with international humanitarian law in its illegal occupation of the Hawaiian islands.* https://www.nlg.org/nlg-calls-upon-us-to-immediately-comply-with-international-humanitarian-law-in-its-illegal-occupation-of-the-hawaiian-islands/

Native American Languages Act. (1990). https://www.govinfo.gov/content/pkg/STATUTE-104/pdf/STATUTE-104-Pg1152.pdf

Native Schools Act 1858. http://www.nzlii.org/nz/legis/hist_act/nsa185821a22v1858n65306/

Native Schools Act 1867. http://www.nzlii.org/nz/legis/hist_act/nsa186731v1867n4129

Néaoutyine, P. (2006). *L'indépendence au present.* EditionsSyllepse.

NeSmith, R. K. (2011). *The teaching and learning of Hawaiian in mainstream educational contexts in Hawai'i: Time for change?* Unpublished doctoral thesis, University of Waikato, New Zealand.

Nettle, D., & Romaine, S. (2000). *Vanishing voices: The extinction of the world's languages.* Oxford University Press.

New Zealand Constitution Act 1852. https://nzhistory.govt.nz/proclamation-of-1852-constitution-act

New Zealand Herald. (2001, January 11). *Editorial: Openness vital to Tainui's recovery.*

Newbury, C. (1973). Resistance and collaboration in French Polynesia: The Tahitian war—1844–7. *Journal of the Polynesian Society, 82*(1), 5–27.

Newbury, C. (1980). *Tahiti nui: Change and survival in French Polynesia, 1767–1945.* University of Hawai'i Press.

Newlands Resolution. (1898). *To provide for Annexing the Hawaiian Islands to the United States.* https://www.bartleby.com/43/44.html

Nock, S. (2010). The reo Māori: Māori language revitalization. In G. Senft (Ed.), *Endangered Austronesian and Australian languages: Essays on language documentation, archiving and revitalization. Pacific Linguistics, 618*, Australian National University.

Nock, S. (2014). *Te whakaako i te reo Māori i te kura auraki tuarua i Aotearoa nei: Kei tua o te awe ampere/The teaching of te reo Māori in English-medium secondary schools in New Zealand: Beyond the mask.* Unpublished doctoral thesis. University of Waikato, New Zealand.

Notting Hill Interiors. (n.d.). http://www.nottinghillinteriors.co.nz/our-story

O'Brien, J. (Producer). (2017, Episode 18). *Hyundai country calendar.* TVNZ 1.

Oliver, D. L. (1974). *Ancient Tahitian society.* University of Hawai'i Press.

Orange, C. (1987). *The treaty of Waitangi.* Bridget Williams Books.

Organic law of 12 April 1996. https://www.legifrance.gouv.fr/affichTexte.do?cidTexte=JORFTEXT000000375561

Ouetcho, C., & Derton, D. (2012). *Nyùwâxè, l'igname amè* [Bitter yam]. ADCK—centre culturel Tjibaou (Nouvelle-Calédonie).

Panelli R, Stolte, O., & Bedford, R. (2003). The reinvention of Tirau: Landscape as a record of changing economy and culture. *Sociologia Ruralis, 43*(4), 379–400.

Pappenhagen, R., Scarvaglieri, C., & Redder, A. (2016). Expanding the linguistic landscape scenery? Action theory and 'linguistic soundscaping'. In R. Blackwood, E. Lanza, & H. Woldemariam (Eds.), *Negotiating and contesting identities in linguistic landscapes* (pp. 147–162). Bloomsbury.

Patterson, M. (n.d.). *How to double your social engagement with images.* Posted under Social Media Marketing. https://www.convinceandconvert.com/social-media-strategy/double-social-engagement-with-images/

Pavlenko, A., & Blackledge, A. (2004). Introduction: New theoretical approaches to the study of negotiation of identities in multilingual contexts. In A. Pavlenko & A. Blackledge (Eds.), *Negotiation of identities in multilingual contexts* (pp. 1–33). Multilingual Matters.

Pennycook, A. (2010). Spatial narrations: Graffscapes and city souls. In A. Jaworski & C. Thurlow (Eds.), *Semiotic landscapes: Language, image, space.* Continuum.

Philippine organic act 1902. https://www.officialgazette.gov.ph/constitutions/the-philippine-organic-act-of-1902/

Pitoiset, A. (2002, October 10). *What is the Tjibaou Centre being used for? Disappointed hopes of the CCT.* L'Express.fr. http://www.lexpres.fr/

Radio New Zealand. (2018, November 19). *Questions about Tahiti nuclear memorial.* https://www.rnz.co.nz/international/pacific-news/376276/questions-about-tahiti-nuclear-memorial

Radio New Zealand. (2019, August 28). *Tenders sought for French Polynesia nuclear testing memorial.* https://www.rnz.co.nz/international/pacific-news/397661/tenders-sought-for-french-polynesia-nuclear-testing-memorial

Ramsay, R. (2011). *Nights of storytelling: A cultural history of Kanaky-New Caledonia.* University of Hawai'i Press.

Razafi, P. E., & Wacalie, F. (2018). Focus sur discriminations linguistiques devenues invisibles. *Palabre, 27*, 46–49.

Recensement de la population 2017: La population légale en Polynésie française au 17 août 2017. http://www.ispf.pf/docs/defaultsource/rp2017/cpo_rp2017.pdf?sfvrs n=2

Reh, M. (2004). Multilingual writing: A reader-oriented typology—With examples from Lira municipality (Uganda). *International Journal of the Sociology of Language, 170*, 1–41.

Rénovation de la Fol: La province dit toujours oui, mais . . . (2014, October 15). https ://www.lnc.nc/breve/renovation-de-la-fol-la-province-dit-toujours-oui-mais

Revised School Laws and Revised Rules and Regulations of the Department of Public Instruction of the Territory of Hawaii. (1905). *Hawaiian Star Print.*

Richardson, M. (2019, August 19). *Parking crackdown, new signs at TMT protest site anger activists.* Hawaii News Now. https://www.hawaiinewsnow.com/2019/08/20/ dot-installs-no-parking-signs-mauna-kea/

Rivas, J. (2018, January 1). *Judge issues arrest warrant to Hawaiian man for speaking his native language in court.* Splinter. https://splinternews.com/judge -issues-arrest-warrant-to-hawaiian-man-for-speakin-1822421239

Rojo, L. M. (2014). Taking over the square: The role of linguistic practices in contesting urban spaces. *Journal of Language and Politics, 13*(4), 624–652.

Rojo, L. M. (Ed.). (2016). *Occupy: The spatial dynamics of discourse in global protest movements.* John Benjamins.

Rouvray (de), L. L. (1946). *Un homme de cran. Guillaume Douarre, premier évêque missionnaire de la Nouvelle-Calédonie.* Beauchesne et son fils.

Rubdy, R., & Ben Said, S. (2015). Conflict and exclusion: The linguistic landscape as an arena of contestation. In R. Rubdy & S. Ben Said (Eds.), *Conflict, exclusion and dissent in the linguistic landscape.* Palgrave Macmillan.

Said, E. (1993). *Culture and imperialism.* Knopf.

Said, S. B., & Kasanga, L. (2016). The discourse of protest: Frames of identity, intertextuality, and interdiscursivity. In R. Blackwood, E. Lanza, & H. Woldemariam (Eds.), *Negotiating and contesting identities in linguistic landscapes* (pp. 721– 783). Bloomsbury.

Salaün, M. (2007). Are Kanak languages to be taught? Social demands and linguistic dilemmas in New Caledonia. *Journal de la Société des Océanistes, 2*, 261–269.

Sallabank, J. (2014). *Language ideologies, practices and policies in New Caledonia.* https://www.youtube.com/watch?v=Q2xbu3JzbBM

Sallabank, J. (2015). Language ideologies, practices and policies in Kanaky/New Caledonia. In M. C. Jones & C. Mari (Ed.), *Language policy for endangered languages* (pp. 31–47). Cambridge University Press.

Salmon, A. (1991). *Two worlds: First meetings between Maori and Europeans 1642–1772.* Viking/Penguin Books.

Salmond, A. (2010). *Aphrodite's island.* Penguin Books.

Samuel, H. (2019, May 24). *France acknowledges Polynesian islands 'strong-armed' into dangerous nuclear tests.* The Telegraph. https://www.telegraph.co.uk/news/20 19/05/24/france-acknowledges-polynesian-islands-strong-armed-dangerous/

Scarvaglieri, C. A., Redder, A., Pappenhagen, R., & Brechmer, B. (2013). Capturing diversity: Linguistic land- and soundscaping in urban areas. In I. Gogolin & J.

Duarte (Eds.), *Linguistic super-diversity in urban areas: Research approaches* (pp. 45–74). Benjamins.

Schafer, M. (1977). *The turning of the world.* Knopf.

Schütz, A. J. (1994). *The voices of Eden: A history of Hawaiian language studies.* University of Hawai'i Press.

Scollon, R., & Scollon, S. W. (2003). *Discourses in place: Language in the material world.* Routledge.

Seabirds. (n.d.). *Koa'e kea or white-tailed tropicbird: Phaethon lepturus.* https://dlnr .hawaii.gov/wildlife/files/2013/09/Fact-Sheet-White-tailed-Tropicbird.pdf

Searle, J. R. (1969). *Speech acts: An essay on the philosophy of language.* Oxford University Press.

Sebba, M. (2010). Book review: Linguistic landscapes: A comparative study of urban multilingualism in Tokyo. *Writing System Research, 2*(1), 73–76.

Shohamy, E. (2006). *Language policy: Hidden agendas and new approaches.* Routledge.

Shohamy, E., & Ghazaleh-Mahajneh, A. (2012). Arabic as a 'minority language' in Israel. In D. Gorter, H. F Marten, & L. Von Mensel (Eds.), *Minority languages in the linguistic landscape.* Palgrave Macmillan.

Shohamy, E., & Gorter, D. (2008). Introduction. In E. Shohamy & D. Gorter (Eds.), *Linguistic landscape: Expanding the scenery* (pp. 1–16). Taylor and Francis.

Shohamy, E., & Waksman, S. (2010). Building the nation, writing the past: History and textuality at the Ha'apala Memorial in Tel Aviv-Jaffa. In A. Jaworski & C. Thurlow (Eds.), *Semiotic landscapes: Language, image, space* (pp. 241–255). Continuum.

Shohamy, E., & Waksman, S. (2012). Talking back to the Tel Aviv centennial: LL responses to top-down agendas. In C. Hélot, M. Barni, R. Janssens, & C. Bagna (Eds.), *Linguistic landscapes, multilingualism and social change* (pp. 109–126). Peter Lang.

Simpson, A. W. B. (2004). *Human rights and the end of empire: Britain and the genesis of the European convention.* Oxford University Press.

Sinclair, K. (1986). *A destiny apart: New Zealand's search for national identity.* Allen & Unwin in association with the Port Nicholson Press.

Smith, L. T. (1999). *Decolonizing methodologies: Research and indigenous peoples.* Zed Books.

Solomon, M. (2015, May 15). *How the debate over TMT prompted a problematic email.* Hawai'i Public Radio. https://www.hawaiipublicradio.org/post/how-debate-over-tmt-prompted-problematic-email#stream/0

Spolsky, B. (2003). Reassessing Māori regeneration. *Language in Society, 32*(4), 553–578.

Spolsky, B., & Cooper, R. L. (1991). *The languages of Jerusalem.* Oxford: Clarendon.

Stanley, D. (2004, December 3). *Lonely planet south pacific.* Moon Handbooks.

Statistics New Zealand. (n.d.). *2013 census data.* http://www.stats.govt.nz/Census /2013-census.aspx?gclid=CMXj99Gfrs8CFUUDvAodmFoD9g

Statute of Westminster 1931. http://www.legislation.gov.uk/ukpga/1931/4/pdfs/ukpga _19310004_en.pdf

Statute of Westminster Adoption Act 1947. http://www.nzlii.org/nz/legis/hist_act/s owaa194711gv1947n38459/

Stewart, P. J., & Strathern, A. (2003). Introduction. In P. J. Stewart & A. Strathern (Eds.), *Landscape, memory and history: Anthropological perspectives* (pp. 1–15). Pluto Press.

Stroud, C. (2016). Turbulent linguistic landscapes and the semiotics of citizenship. In R. E. L. Blackwood & H. Woldemariam (Eds.), *Negotiating and contesting identities in linguistic landscapes.* Bloomsbury.

Tahiti's Independence Movement Revives. (1995, July 26). *Green Left Weekly, 195.* https://www.greenleft.org.au/content/tahitis-independence-movement-revives

Taylor, K., & Lennon, J. L. (2012). Introduction: Leaping the fence. In K. Taylor & J. L. Lennon (Eds.), *Managing cultural landscapes.* Routledge.

Te Ara: The encyclopedia of New Zealand (n.d.). *Population.* https://www.stats.govt .nz/topics/population

Te Tiriti o Waitangi/Treaty of Waitangi, 1840. http;//www.treatyofwaitangi.maori.nz

Tetiartahi,. G. (1987). The society islands: Squeezing out the Polynesians. In R. Crocombe (Ed.), *Land tenure in the Pacific* (pp. 45–58). University of the South Pacific.

The Tjibaou cultural centre and ADCK, prēsentation. http://www.adck.nc/presentatio n/english-presentation/the-tjibaou-cultural-centre-and-adck

Thistlethwaite, J., & Sebba, R. (2015). The passive exclusion of Irish in the linguistic landscape: A nexus analysis. In R. Rubdy & S. Ben Said (Eds.), *Conflict, exclusion and dissent in the linguistic landscape.* Palgrave Macmillan.

Tirau info. (n.d.). http://www.tirauinfo.co.nz/html/tirau_s_past.html

Torfing, J. (2005). Discourse theory: Achievements, arguments, and challenges. In D. Howarth & J. Torfing (Eds.), *Discourse theory in European politics: Identity, policy and governance* (pp. 1–32). Palgrave.

Tourism New Zealand. (n.d.). *About the tourist industry.* http://www.tourismnewzeal and.com/about/about-the-industry/m%C4%81ori-tourism/

Toyota Hillux Advertisement. (n.d.). http://www.teara.govt.nz/en/video/22432/toyot a-hilux-advertisement-1999

Treaty of Hawaii 1900. An Act to provide a government for the territory of Hawaii. https://www.loc.gov/law/help/statutes-at-large/56th-congress/session-1/c56s1ch33 9.pdf

Treaty of Manilla. https://en.wikisource.org/wiki/Treaty_of_Manila_(1946)

Treaty of Paris 1898. https://en.wikisource.org/wiki/Treaty_of_Paris_(1898)

Tripadvisor, New Zealand: Noumea. https://www.tripadvisor.co.nz/Tourism-g2 94130-Noumea_Grand_Terre-Vacations.html

UN Convention on the Law of the Sea. (1982). https://www.un.org/depts/los/conven tion_agreements/texts/unclos/unclos_e.pdf

United Nations. (1960). *Declaration on the granting of independence to colonial countries and peoples.* https://www.refworld.org/docid/3b00f06e2f.html

United Nations. (2008). *Declaration on the rights of indigenous peoples.* https://ww w.un.org/development/desa/indigenouspeoples/wp-content/uploads/sites/19/2018 /11/UNDRIP_E_web.pdf

United Nations Convention on the Law of the Sea (1982, December 10; enacted 1994, November 1). https://www.un.org/depts/los/convention_agreements/texts/unclos/u nclos_e.pdf

United Nations Educational, Scientific and Cultural Organization. *Atlas of the world's languages in danger.* http://www.unesco.org/languages-atlas/

United Nations Office for Disarmament Affairs. (n.d.). *Comprehensive nuclear test-ban treaty.* https://www.un.org/disarmament/wmd/nuclear/ctbt/

US Census. (1896). *Statistical abstract of the United States: 1896.* https://www.cen sus.gov/library/publications/1897/compendia/statab/19ed.html

US Census. (2010). *Decennial census of population and housing.* https://www.census .gov/programs-surveys/decennial-census/decade.2010.html

Vale, L. J. (1999, Winter). Mediated monuments and national identity. *The Journal of Architecture, 4*, 391–408.

Van Dijk, J. M. (2007). *Who owns the crown lands of Hawai'i ?* University of Hawai'i Press.

Van Dijk, M. B. (2019, August 17). *'A new Hawaiian Renaissance': How a telescope protest became a movement.* The Guardian (International Edition). https://www.theguardian.com/us-news/2019/aug/16/hawaii-telescope-protest-ma una-kea

Waitangi Tribunal. (1986). *Report of the Waitangi Tribunal on the te reo Maori claim.* Department of Justice (NZ). https://forms.justice.govt.nz/search/Document s/WT/wt_DOC_68482156/Report%20on%20the%20Te%20Reo%20Maori%20 Claim%20W.pdf

Waitangi Tribunal. (2001). *Ko Aotearoa tēnei: A report into claims concerning New Zealand law and policy affecting Māori culture and identity. Wai 262. Taumata* II, Vol. 2. Legislation Direct. https://waitangitribunal.govt.nz/news/ko-aotearoa-tenei -report-on-the-wai-262-claim-released/

Waksman, S., & Shohamy, E. (2016), Linguistic landscape of social protests: Moving from 'open' to 'institutional' spaces. In R. Blackwood, E. Lanza, & H. Woldemariam (Eds.), *Negotiating and contesting identities in linguistic landscapes.* Bloomsbury.

Walk, K. (2008). Officially' what? The legal rights and implications of Ōlelo Hawai'i. *University of Hawai'i Law Review, 243*, 250. https://www.mokuolahonua.com/r esources/language-policy-and-advocacy/2019/2/18/officially-what-the-legal-rights -and-implications-of-lelo-hawaii-yk9gg

Walker, R. (2004). *Ka whawhai tonu mātou: Struggle without end.* Penguin.

Wallace, N. (2014). *When the gates opened: The impact of Rogernomics on rural New Zealand.* Otago University Press.

Wang, F. K.-H. (2018, March 1). *Hawaiian language finds new prominence in Hawaii's courts decades after near disappearance.* NBC News Online. https:// www.nbcnews.com/news/asian-america/hawaiian-language-finds-new-prominenc e-hawaii-s-courts-decades-after-n851536

Watson, M. (2019, March 15). *Christchurch mosque terrorism attack IS New Zealand's most deadly shooting.* Stuff. https://www.stuff.co.nz/national/1113215 23/worst-shootings-on-record

Webb, M., & Webb-Gannon, C. (2018, October 31). *Rebel music: The protest songs of New Caledonia's independence referendum*. The Conversation. http://theconve rsation.com/rebel-music-the-protest-songs-of-new-caledonias-independence-re ferendum-105580

Weekend Herald. (2016, February 6). *Mana and money*.

Westervelt, W. D. (1999). *Hawaiian legends of ghosts and ghost-gods*. Mutual Pub.

Weyler, R. (2004). *Greenpeace: How a group of ecologists, journalists, and visionaries changed the world*. Rodale.

Wilmshurst, J. M., Hunt, T. L., Lipoc, C. P., & Anderson, A. J. (2011, February 1). High-precision radiocarbon dating shows recent and rapid initial human colonization of East Polynesia. *Proceedings of the National Academy of Sciences (PNAS)*. https://www.pnas.org/content/108/5/1815

Winslow, D. (1991, June). Land and independence in New Caledonia. *Cultural Survival Quarterly Magazine, 15*(2). https://www.culturalsurvival.org/publications /cultural-survival-quarterly/land-and-independence-new-caledonia

Wodak, R. (2001). What CDA is about. In R. Wodak & M. Meyer (Eds.), *Methods of critical discourse analysis*. SAGE.

Wolfe, P. (2006). Settler colonialism and the elimination of the native. *Journal of Genocide Research, 8*(4), 387–409.

World Conference on Linguistic Rights. (1996). *Universal declaration of linguistic rights* (Beatriu Krayenbühl i Gusi: Trans.). https://culturalrights.net/descargas/dre ts_culturals389.pdf

Wylie, J. (2007). *Landscape*. Routledge.

Zweifel, W. (2018, November 9). *Where to next for New Caledonia?* Radio New Zealand Pacific report. https://www.rnz.co.nz/international/pacific-news/375536/ where-to-next-for-new-caledonia

Zweifel, W. (2019, June 4). *Stalled nuclear compensation irks Tahitian claimants*. Radio New Zealand. https://www.rnz.co.nz/international/pacific-news/391196/stal led-nuclear-compensation-irks-tahiti-claimants

Index

agriculture, 1, 21, 50, 96
Alexandre, F., 98
The Alley Cats Café, 59, 60
Anaya, James, 75
Antiques @ Tirau, 59–60
Aotearoa/New Zealand study, 13;
    background of location and
    population, 47–50; corrugated
    iron and, 52, 54–55, 59–60, 63,
    65–66; indigenous people in, 50–52;
    linguistic landscape in study site,
    55–66; myth and, 52, 66; national
    identity and, 14; site selection, 52–
    55. *See also* Māori language; Māori
    people; Tirau, New Zealand
Arden, Jacinda, 8
Arvin, Maile, 31–32, 46n16
Asuncion, Keola, 39, *41*, *42*, *43*
Atlas of Endangered Languages
    (UNESCO), 76
Avenue Bruat, 107
Avenue Clémenceau, 103
Avenue du Prince Hinoi, 102–3

Bachimon, P., 101
Backhaus, P., 4
Balfour Declaration, 49
Bensa, Alban, 78, 80, 90n6
Ben Said, S., 7

bilingualism, 10; of Māori people, 51;
    Tahitian people and, 98; in Wales, 11
Blackwood, R. J., 6
Bligh, William, 94
body art: Hawaiian Kingdom/Hawai'i
    study and, 34–36; language in, *36*
Bougainville, Louis-Antoine de, 94
Boulevard Pomare, 108
Bounty, HMS, 104
Bourhis, R. Y., 4
Britain, 20; colonialism of, 3, 17, 122;
    in European Economic Community,
    14, 53, 67n7, 122; expansionism
    of, 17; Hawaiian Kingdom and, 30;
    Māori people and, 49; New Zealand
    and, 48
Brown, Peter, 80
Bruat, Armand Joseph, 107
The Bugger Café, 59–60, *60*

Cameron, D., 14
CCT. *See* Jean-Marie Tjibaou Cultural
    Center
CDT. *See* critical discourse theory
Charpentier, J.-M., 98
Chastenet de Géry, Jean, 105
Chirac, Jacques, 99
Christian, Fletcher, 94
Christianity, 1, 20, 75, 95, 97, 108

Cleveland, Grover, 22
Colette, Juste François, 107
collective gaze, 14
colonialism: of Britain, 3, 17, 122; of France, 69–72; Hawaiian Kingdom/Hawai'i study and, 32–34; Māori people and, 49, 122–23; Maunakea mountain protest against, 32–43; of United States, 3, 18, 122. *See also* expansionism
Commonwealth of Nations, 17, 49
Comprehensive Nuclear-Test-Ban Treaty, 99
Contemporary Pacific, 80
Cook, James, 19, 48, 74, 94
Cooper, R. L., 6
corrugated iron, 52, 54–55, 59–60, 63, 65–66
COVID-19 pandemic, 125
critical discourse theory (CDT), 44; relevance of, 7–10; research methods and, 10–11; social structures and, 6–7; for study perspective, 12
Crown Lands, 30, 38
culture: cultural diversity loss, 125; of indigenous peoples of Pacific, 2; of Kanak people, 80–81; subcultures, 7; of Tahitian people, 96–97; Tahitian study and, 96–97

deforestation, 125
De Gaulle, Charles, 70, 98, 102, 105, 123
Democratic rally of the Tahitian people (*Rassemblement démocratique des populations tahitiennes*), 102
Destremau, Maxime, 104–5
de Zayas, A. M., 27–28
Douglas, Roger, 67n7
D'Urville, Jules Sébastien César Dumont, 105–6

Edge of Empire (Jacobs), 115
EEC. *See* European Economic Community

English language: Maunakea mountain protest and, 28–38, *29, 32, 35, 41, 42, 42*; signs in, 37–38, *110,* 110–12, *111, 112,* 124
European Charter for Regional and Minority Languages, 71
European Economic Community (EEC), 14, 53, 67n7, 122
expansionism: of Britain, 17; of France, 69–72; of United states, 3, 18, 122

Facebook, 8, 44–45
Fairclough, Norman, 10
Federation of Lay Works (FOL): deterioration of, 81–82, 90, 123; graffiti on, 14, 82–87, *83, 84, 85,* 90, 123; linguistic landscape of, 82–87, 123
Ferry, Jules, 69
fishing, 1, 23, 100
Flosse, Gaston, 99
FLP. *See* Front for the Liberation of Polynesia
FOL. *See* Federation of Lay Works
France, 48; attitude toward language in territories, 70–72; colonialism and expansionism, 69–72; extent of empire, 59–60; French Union in, 69; future importance of possessions, 72; overseas regions and overseas collectives, 69–70
Free French movement, 101, 103, 105, 108
Freeman, James, 48
French language: Kanak people speaking, 86; monolingualism, 98; signs in, *110,* 110–12, *111, 112,* 124
French Polynesia, 70, 72, 93–94, 96–99, 101–5; languages, 118n7
Fritch, Edouard, 100, 124
Front for the Liberation of Polynesia (FLP), 102

globalization, 7–8, 44, 112, 121, 125
global warming, 125

graffiti: on Federation of Lay Works, 14, 82–87, *83*, *84*, *85*, 90, 123; at Maunakea mountain, 41; social disquiet signaled by, 15

Ha'apala Memorial, Tel Aviv-Jaffa, 14
Hall, S., 7
The Handle Bar, 59–60
Hawaii Admissions Act, 22
Hawaiian Homes commission Act, 22
Hawaiian Islands: Bayonet Constitution in, 21; Hawaiian Kingdom established, 20–21; hazardous materials in, 23; illegal occupation of, 45; indigenous people of, 23–26; Kingdom overthrow in, 21–22; location and first settlements in, 19–20; as military base, 23; recognition of Kingdom, 45n2; traditional religion on, 23
Hawaiian Kingdom/Hawai'i study, 121–22; body art and, 34–36, *35*; Britain and, 30; changing linguistic landscape at Maunakea mountain, 28–32; Crown Lands and, 30, 38; exploration of linguistic landscape in, 26–43; illegal occupation of Hawaiian Kingdom and, 31; indigenous people in, 23–26; overview of Hawaiian Islands and people, 19–26; protest against colonialism, 32–34; protest signs in Hawaiian language, *38*, 38–43, *40*, *41*; protest site, 13, 26–28; public space and, 12–13; war dance performance and, 39; YouTube and, 36–37. *See also* Maunakea mountain; Native Hawaiians
Hawaiian language: *ka ōlelo Hawai'i* language, 25; *ōlelo Hawai'i* language, 23–24; protest signs in, *38*, 38–43, *40*, *41*
Hedley, Rangiiria, 81
hegemony, 7–8, 19
Herman, D., 27

Hobson, William, 48
Hughes, G., 55

identity: Aotearoa/New Zealand study and, 14; linguistic landscape and, 7; of Māori people, 52; signs and, 11; tourism and, 14
indigenous people: in Aotearoa/New Zealand study, 50–52; colonization and reclamation, 3–4; culture and language, 2; in Hawaiian Kingdom/Hawai'i study, 23–26; International Year of Indigenous Languages (2019), 124; in Kanaky/New Caledonia study, 74–76; origins of, 1–2. *See also* Kanak people; Māori people; Native Hawaiians; Tahitian people
International Year of Indigenous Languages (2019), 124
Internet, 12, 60

Jacobs, Jane, 115
Jaussen, Florentin-Étienne, 107
Jaworski, A., 5, 14, 15
Jean-Marie Tjibaou Cultural Center (CCT), *79*; design of, 78–79; Kanak culture and, 80–81; linguistic landscape of, 14, 87–90, 123; mission of, 79–80; opening of, 84; signs in, *88*, 88–89, *89*
Jefferson, T., 7
Jolly, Margaret, 80
Jones, R. H., 13
Journal of Language and Politics, 13

Ka'eoa, Samuel Kaleikoa, 25–26
Kahn, M., 101
Kalākaua (King), 21
Kamehameha I, 20
Kamehameha II, 20
Kamehameha III, 20; on protest signs, 41, *43*
Kamehameha IV, 20–21
Kamehameha V, 21, 29

Kanak language, 86, 123; signs in, 88–89, 91n10; 28 varieties of, 76

Kanak people, 72, 90n1; clan affiliation among, 74–75; collapse of society, 83; creation legends of, 87; cultural display at Jean-Marie Tjibaou Cultural Center, 80–81; culture of, 80–81; French spoken by, 86; independence movement of, 74, 77–78; poverty among, 75

Kanaky/New Caledonia study: exploring linguistic landscape in, 78–89; Federation of Lay Works and, 14; indigenous people in, 74–76; language and, 76; location and occupation in, 73–74; public space in, 14–15. *See also* Federation of Lay Works; Jean-Marie Tjibaou Cultural Center; Kanak language; Kanak people

Kasanga, L., 11, 12

Kasarhérou, Emmanuel, 80–81

Kerr, Tom, 27

LaGarde, Auguste Felix, 105

land alienation, 18

Landry, R., 4

language: in body art, *36*; *European Charter for Regional and Minority Languages*, 71; of French Polynesia, 118n7; in French territories, 70–72; of indigenous peoples of Pacific, 2; Kanaky/New Caledonia study and, 76; linguistic diversity loss, 125; Marquesian language, 97–98; Native Hawaiians and, 38; New Zealand sign language, 47; Tayo language, 76. *See also* bilingualism; English language; French language; Hawaiian language; Kanak language; Māori language; Tahitian language

Law concerning overseas adaptation 2000 (La loi d'orientation pour l'outre-mer 2000), 71

League of Nations, 49, 67n6

Levy, Robert, 98

Liliʻuokalani (Queen), 21–23, 45n3, 46n24

linguistic landscape (LL): in Aotearoa/New Zealand study site, 55–66; changing, at Maunakea mountain, 28–32; exploration in Hawaiian Kingdom/Hawaiʻi study, 26–43; exploration in Kanaky/New Caledonia study, 78–89; exploration in Papeʻete, Tahiti, 102–15; exploration in Tahitian study, 102–15; of Federation of Lay Works, 14, 82–87, 123; hegemony and, 7–8, 10; identity and, 7; introduction to studies, 11–15; at Jean-Marie Tjibaou Cultural Center, 14, 87–90, 123; private, 16n9; signs and, 4–5; study of, 4–7; in Tirau commercial area, 55–66

La loi d'orientation pour l'outre-mer 2000 (Law concerning overseas adaptation 2000), 71

La loi Toubon, 111

Losche, D., 80

Louis Philippe I, 108

Lunalilo (King), 21

Maastricht Treaty, 71

Macalister, J., 52

Macron, Emmanuel, 78

Malinovsky, Michel, 85–86

Maohi people, 72

Māori language, 8–10, 47–49; decline of, 50–51; Māori Language Act of 1987, 52; possession and protection of, 51–52; street names in, 56; on Tirau signs, 61–62

Māori people, 16n2; bilingualism, 51; Britain and, 49; colonialism and, 49, 122–23; genealogy and, 50; lack of heritage in Tirau, 66–67; New Zealand identity and, 52; pepper-potting of, 51; poverty among,

50–52; tourism and, 55, 122; villages of, 53

Markus, T. A., 14

Marquesian language, 97–98

Marten, H. F., 44

Matignon Agreements, 77–79

Maunakea mountain, 12, 121–22, 124; body art signs, 34–36, *35*; changing linguistic landscape at, 28–32; extension of protest, 44; graffiti at, 41; Native Hawaiians and, 26–31, 39–40, 43–44; no parking signs, 32–33, *33*; police presence at, 33–34, *34*; protest against colonialism, 32–43; protest signs in English, 28–38, *29, 32, 35, 41*, 42, *42*; protest signs in Hawaiian language, *38*, 38–43, *40, 41*; as study site, 13, 26–28; war dance performance, 39

Mauna Kea Science Reserve, 26–27

McKinley, William, 22

McKinley Tariff, 45n3

The Merchant of Tirau, 57–60, *59*

Message, K., 79–80

Mills, Antonia, 35

mise en abyme effect, 28

Momoa, Jason, 34, *35*, 47n17

monolingualism, 98

Monroe Doctrine, 1821, 18

multi-modal approach, 5

National Lawyers Guild, 45

Native Americans Languages Act (1990), 25

Native Hawaiians, 12, 20–23; language and, 38; Maunakea mountain and, 26–31, 39–40, 43–44

Nettle, D., 1

New Caledonia, 69–72; nickel in, 75, 77. *See also* Kanaky/New Caledonia study

New Zealand: Britain and, 48; identity and Māori people, 52; New Zealand Company, 48; New Zealand Constitution Act, 49; New Zealand

sign language, 47; Rogernomics in, 67n7; tourism in, 68n8. *See also* Aotearoa/New Zealand study

Al Noor Mosque attack, 8

Notting Hill Interiors, 57, 59

Nouméa Accord, 78, 90n4

nuclear testing: *Comprehensive Nuclear-Test-Ban Treaty*, 99; deaths from, 99–100, 115; Pā'ōfa'i Gardens Nuclear Testing Memorial Site, 115, *116, 117*, 118; Tahitian study and, 98–100, 115–16, 123–24

Oceania, 1

Okoroire Street, 56

'Ō'opa, Pouvāna'a Tetuaapua, 101–3

overseas collectives, 69–70

overseas regions, 69–70

The Oxford Café, 57–58, *58*, 60

Oxford Street, 56

Pacific Islands Forum (PIF), 72

Panelli R., 55

Pā'ōfa'i Gardens Nuclear Testing Memorial Site, 115, *116, 117*, 118

Pape'ete, Tahiti, 15; exploration of linguistic landscape, 102–15; Pā'ōfa'i Gardens Nuclear Testing Memorial Site, 115, *116, 117*, 118; signs for commercial establishments, 109–15, *110, 111, 112, 114*, 124, 125; street names in, 102–9, *104*, 116–17; as study site, 102–3; threats to, 102

Pappenhagen, R., 11, 15

Piano, Renzo, 78

PIF. *See* Pacific Islands Forum

Place Notre Dame, 107

Pōmare II, 95, 101

Pōmare III, 95

Pōmare IV, 95–96, 106, 108

Pōmare V, 96, 107, 108

Pōmare Legal Code, 95

population: in Aotearoa/New Zealand study, 47–50; population explosion, 125

poverty: of Kanak people, 75; of Māori people, 50–52; of Tahitian people, 100–101

public space, 12–13, 15

Rassemblement démocratique des populations tahitiennes (Democratic rally of the Tahitian people), 102

Reciprocity Treaty of 1875, 45n3

Redder, A., 15

Rogernomics, 67n7

Rojo, L. M., 13, 44

Romaine, S., 1

Rubdy, R., 7

Rue Colette, 107

Rue Cook, 103

Rue de Anne-Marue Jovouhey, 107

Rue de Commandant Destremeau, 105

Rue de La Cannonière Zélée, 104

Rue de L'Arthémise, 106

Rue des Poilus Tahitiens, 103, 104, 107

Rue des Remparts, 103

Rue du 22 Septembre, 104

Rue du Chef Teriierooitera, 108

Rue du General de Gaulle, 103, 106

Rue du Maréchal Foch, 103

Rue Dumont D'Urville, 103, 105–6

Rue du Petit Thouars, 106–7

Rue Edouard Ahnne, 105

Rue François Cardella, 107

Rue Jeanne d'Arc, 103, *104*

Rue Lagarde, 105

Rue Mgr T. Jauseen, 107

Said, E., 11, 12

Salmond, A., 96

Scarvaglieri, C. A., 15

Schütz, A. J., 24–25

Scollon, R., 5

Scollon, S. W., 5

semiotoscape, 5, 13, 66

Shohamy, E., 12, 14

signs: for commercial establishments, Pape'ete, Tahiti, 109–15, *110, 111, 112, 114*, 125; in English, *110*, 110–12, *111, 112*, 124; in French, *110*, 110–12, *111, 112*, 124; in Gambian souvenir market, 14; identity and, 11; in Jean-Marie Tjibaou Cultural Center, 87–89, *88, 89*; Kamehameha III pictured on, 41, *43*; in Kanak language, 88–89, 91n10; linguistic landscape and, 4–5; Māori language on, *61*, 61–62, *62*; at Pā'ōfa'i Gardens Nuclear Testing Memorial Site, 115, *116, 117*; protest signs in English, 28–38, *29, 32, 35, 41*, 42, *42*; protest signs in Hawaiian language, *38*, 38–43, *40, 41*; staging of, 36, *37*; in Tahitian language, 117; in Tirau, New Zealand, 13–14, 55, 61–62

Sisters of Saint Joseph of Cluny, 107

Société des missions évangéliques de Paris, 95–96, 105

soundscape, 5, 16n5

Spolsky, B., 6

Statute of Westminster, 49

street names: *Avenue Bruat*, 107; *Avenue Clémenceau*, 103; *Avenue du Prince Hinoi*, 102–3; *Boulevard Pomare*, 108; in Māori language, 56; *Okoroire Street*, 56; *Oxford Street*, 56; in Pape'ete, Tahiti, 102–9, *104*, 116–17; *Place Notre Dame*, 107; *Rose Street*, 56; *Rue Colette*, 107; *Rue Cook*, 103; *Rue de Anne-Marue Jovouhey*, 107; *Rue de Commandant Destremeau*, 105; *Rue de La Cannonière Zélée*, 104; *Rue de L'Arthémise*, 106; *Rue des Poilus Tahitiens*, 103, 104, 107; *Rue des Remparts*, 103; *Rue du 22 Septembre*, 104; *Rue du Chef Teriierooitera*, 108; *Rue du General de Gaulle*, 106; *Rue du Maréchal Foch*, 103; *Rue Dumont D'Urville*,

103, 105–6; *Rue du Petit Thouars*, 106–7; *Rue Edouard Ahnne*, 105; *Rue François Cardella*, 107; *Rue Jeanne d'Arc*, 103; *Rue Lagarde*, 105; *Rue Mgr T. Jauseen*, 107; in Tirau, New Zealand, 56
Stroud, C., 11
subcultures, 7
suicide, 122

Tagupa, William, 25
Tahitian language, 39, 97–98; on commercial signs, 117, 124; numbers of speakers, 110; at Pā'ōfa'i Gardens Nuclear Testing Memorial Site, 118; survival of, 124
Tahitian people: bilingualism and, 98; culture of, 96–97; deaths from nuclear testing, 99–100, 115; poverty and alienation of, 100–101; resistance by, 101–2
Tahitian study, 15; culture and, 96–97; exploration of linguistic landscape, 102–15; interviews in, 112, *113*, 114; location for, 93–96; nuclear testing and, 98–100, 115–16, 123–24; tourism and, 100–101. *See also* Pape'ete, Tahiti; Tahitian people
Tasman, Abel, 48
Tayo language, 76
Téâ Kanaké, 78, 87
Temaru, Oscar, 98, 99, 102, 115
Teri'iero'o a Teri'iero'oitera'i, 108
30-meter telescope (TMT), 27–28, 44
Thouars, Abel du Petit, 106–7
Thurlow, C., 5, 14, 15
Tirau, New Zealand, *54*; fantasy-scape in, 67; lack of heritage of Māori people, 66–67; linguistic landscape in commercial area, 55–66; Māori images and language on signs, *61*, 61–62, *62*; myth and, 66; names for commercial establishments, 56–60, *57*; shop sign images in, 60–61; signs in, 13–14, 55; street names in, 56;

as study site, 52–55; suicide in, 122; tourism in, 53–55; visitor interviews in, 63–64, *64*; whimsical commercial presentation in, *62*, 62–63, *65*, 65–66
Tirau's Outhouse, *65*, 65–66
Tjibaou, Jean-Marie, 74, 79–80
TMT. *See* 30-meter telescope
tourism: Māori people and, 55, 122; national identity and, 14; in New Zealand, 68n8; in Pacific Islands, 1; Tahitian study and, 100–101; in Tirau, New Zealand, 53–55
Truthout, 31–32
Tufi, S., 6
turbulence, 16n6, 116

United Nations, 67n6; Office of the High Commissioner for Human Rights, 27; UNESCO, 76; *United Nations Declaration on the Granting of Independence to Colonial Countries and Peoples*, 3; *United Nations Declaration on the Rights of Indigenous Peoples*, 3–4
United States (US), 20, 48; colonialism and expansionism, 3, 18, 122; territories of, 18
Universal Declaration of Linguistic Rights, 3

Vale, Lawrence, 80–81

Waikato-Tainui settlement, 9–10
Waitangi, Treaty of, 48–51
Waksman, S., 12, 14
Wallis, Samuel, 94
war dance performance, 39
Williams, Henry, 48
Wodak, Ruth, 10

YouTube, 36–37

Zélée gunboat, 104–5

About the Author

Dr. Diane Johnson was a linguist/applied linguist/discourse analyst who studied, lived, and worked in a variety of locations throughout Europe, Asia, and Oceania, always immersing herself in the local languages and cultures. As a teacher in Kanaky/New Caledonia, she sang with a group of Kanaky musicians; as a lecturer at *The University of Waikato* in Aoteaoroa/New Zealand, she worked closely with Māori friends and colleagues, acting as a member of the editorial board of *The Journal of Māori and Pacific Development* and supervising the research of many doctoral scholars from around the world whose focus was on indigenous, community, and international languages; as a visiting professor at *Wenzao Ursuline University of Languages* in Taiwan, she worked with local scholars to design culturally focused language learning materials. She was deeply committed to the provision of quality education, providing educational advisory services in Asia and Oceania and playing a major role in the design of national languages curricula in Aotearoa. For many years, she was Chair of the Board of Governors of *Hamilton Girls' High School* in Aotearoa (where she taught for several years following her graduate studies in France). Her innovative and dynamic university-level teaching was recognized in local and national (Aotearoa) teaching excellence awards.